Creative Ideas for Assessing Vulnerable Children and Families

Creative Ideas for Assessing Vulnerable Children and Families

KATIE WRENCH

Jessica Kingsley *Publishers*
London and Philadelphia

Table i.1 reproduced from Horwath (2010) with permission.
List on pages 37–38 reproduced from Rose (2012) with permission.
List on pages 129–130 reproduced from Dalzell and Sawyer (2016) with permission.
Table 6.1 reproduced from Hasler (2017) with permission.

First published in 2018
by Jessica Kingsley Publishers
73 Collier Street
London N1 9BE, UK
and
400 Market Street, Suite 400
Philadelphia, PA 19106, USA

www.jkp.com

Library of Congress Cataloging in Publication Data
A CIP catalog record for this book is available from the Library of Congress

British Library Cataloguing in Publication Data
A CIP catalogue record for this book is available from the British Library

ISBN 978 1 84905 703 5
eISBN 978 1 78450 225 6

Printed and bound in Great Britain

Acknowledgements

Heartfelt thanks are due to many people in enabling this book to come into being…it has been such a long road.

Thank you to Steve Jones and colleagues at Jessica Kingsley Publishers for your patience, support and professionalism. I think collectively we have done a great job.

Thank you to Alison Ferguson for spending time with me on two writing breaks down in West Sussex; for keeping me going with coffee, good food and words of encouragement. Also for being, as ever, the grammar police and making sure what I've written is straightforward for anyone to understand.

Thank you to Jo Robinson, my second critical friend and shining new star in our team of therapeutic social workers. I hope this book becomes the social work 'bible' you predict.

Thank you to my family – to Stephen, Louis and Honor, who have tolerated my absences both physical and psychological, as this book has been written. I promise no more! Stephen, now it's your turn.

Finally, this book is dedicated to the memory of my friend and colleague Athaliah Durrant. She inspired me and many, many others, with her generosity of spirit, her creativity and her focus on making absolutely certain every child she met knew how special they were. She is missed every day, but stays with me through the homemade toy bags she so kindly gifted me when I first joined the team. Love and thanks from your 'green-eyed, blonde-haired girl' – and 'yes, I still work here'.

Contents

INTRODUCTION[1]

Assessments of vulnerable children and families are often required in challenging circumstances and with a requirement to be completed within very tight timescales. Ideally, we need a wide lens through which to consider their individual needs, but so often become involved following a crisis event, which narrows the focus onto securing immediate safety. Assessments can inevitably become incident-driven when they ought to focus more broadly on how to improve outcomes for children and their families, enabling children to meet their potential *as well as* securing safety if necessary. We can only do this by reaching robust, evidence-informed formulations,[2] that can in turn lead to effective plans and interventions.

> Good formulation is often built on a premise that, at essence, people make sense. All individuals function in the way that they function for a reason…the understanding of the *why* leads naturally to an awareness of *what*, along with the flexible capacity to explore *how*. (Blaustein and Kinniburgh 2010, p.46)

We can only reach sound formulations when we holistically understand what is happening day to day in children and their family's lives.

---

1   Please note that throughout this book, for simplicity, I refer to children and young people using masculine pronouns as it can feel cumbersome to be reading he/she, his/her, etc. Similarly, I largely refer to parents or caregivers rather than mothers/fathers. Please take no meaning from this and know I am referring to girls/boys and mothers/fathers in equal measure. Where there are gender-specific differences, I refer to these as appropriate.

2   Namely, the integration of all the information gathered throughout an assessment, such as family history, observations, behaviours, relational style, environmental and social factors.

If we just look to the outcome (e.g. poor school attendance) without understanding the context and the driver for the behaviour (the young person is a carer for a single parent with mental health difficulties), then it is likely that our intervention plan will be less effective and outcomes less positive.

However, when we feel under pressure to complete assessments swiftly, our time, resources, energy and sometimes our motivation are depleted. This is when our creativity and empathy can also become sidelined. For diverse reasons, *we need to get the job done* as quickly as we can, and within such a context it can feel as if there is simply not enough time to be creative in our work with children and families. When practitioners are feeling overwhelmed, it can be harder to comprehend how working creatively or even non-verbally could possibly yield the information we need in the timeliest manner, and lead to better outcomes for families.

Whilst I expect this book will be useful for practitioners across diverse fields, because my core training is in social work it is inevitable that in thinking about creative assessments with vulnerable families and their children, there will be a social care bias, but please keep an open mind if this is not your field. The thematic approach to the chapters means that the exercises can be adapted across many assessment contexts for unique children and families in their own unique milieu. In social work, it is the *Framework for the Assessment of Children in Need and their Families* (DoH 2000) that provides us with a map to shape our thinking in social work assessments. This framework is organised into three domains representing critical components of the child's internal and external worlds, comprising:

- the child's developmental needs
- family and environmental factors
- parenting capacity.

But irrespective of the framework within which you are practising, assessments should never be simply a static, paper exercise. Horwath talks about assessment as 'a relational activity' (Horwath 2010 p.43); as an assessor you are a critical component in the process and can heavily influence the outcome. Even in the most urgent of circumstances, where risks to safety can feel intolerably high, the quality of our interactions with children and families can influence the outcome, both positively and negatively. Effective relationships between practitioners, children and their families increase the likelihood of a commitment from all parties to meet the needs of the child. As practitioners, we need to think about how we use ourselves as a resource, in recognition of the fact that the quality and outcome of any assessment is significantly affected by our success in actively engaging the child and family (Horwath 2010, p.61).

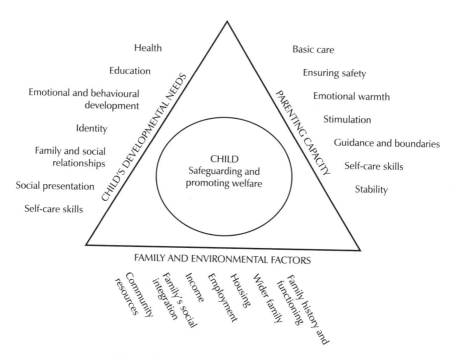

Figure i.1 The Assessment Framework
(Department of Health et al. 2000)

Yet, in such contexts, there will always be a power imbalance between the practitioner, the child and the family. It is essential therefore to create the optimum conditions in which children and their families feel both confident and safe enough to express their views and share their lives with us. In my experience, offering a creative, collaborative assessment approach, without sole focus on the spoken word, provides a less threatening experience that will ultimately contribute to better outcomes for children and their families. By developing our own creative resources as practitioners, we can challenge practice that puts children and young people on the receiving end of adult-centred communication. Where we fail to develop the depth of relationships necessary to safeguard children, children are inevitably not safeguarded. We must be convinced that we will gain insight by listening to children's experiences, otherwise we are unlikely to 'truly engage with their voices in anything other than in tokenistic ways' (Dunhill, Elliot and Shaw 2009, p.40).

This book is therefore motivated by two prime factors. One of my main concerns when it comes to social work assessments relates to an over-reliance on expecting children and families to *talk* about traumatic or distressing events. Whilst there are many elements that influence the efficacy of an assessment, I am concerned about the quality of the information we gather when we prioritise verbal communication and what this then means in terms of outcomes for vulnerable children and their families. In this book, I will offer many creative activities as an alternative to, or to facilitate, verbal interviews for adults and children, as well as exploring why it can be so hard, if not impossible at times, for traumatised individuals to talk to you about what has happened to them.

The second motivator is a very practical one: how best to gain knowledge and understanding of the child and his caregiving system that allows us to undertake effective, child-centred assessments within very real practical constraints; of time, experience, confidence and potentially resistance. The *Framework for the Assessment of Children in Need and their Families* (DoH 2000) is explicit about the need to: *see* the child; *observe* the child; *engage with* the child; *talk with* the child; and *do activities with* the child (my italics). However, it's clear to me that as practitioners we don't always have as much time as we might like to spend planning direct work sessions and gathering together resources. We can be 'constrained by excessive levels of case recording and other bureaucracy, tight timescale for completing work, high caseloads, and compliance with procedures and management dictates' (Ferguson, 2016, p.3). We may have very limited time to build relationships with children and families who might not feel trust in professionals; it is essential therefore to have confidence in the direct work tools we use and to have a range of resources that will meet the diverse communication needs of children and their families.

In over 20 years supporting vulnerable children and young people as a residential care officer, social worker, foster carer and art psychotherapist, I have developed a tried and tested toolkit of ideas and activities, but in the moment, when under pressure I can still struggle to recall an appropriate exercise to use or else risk becoming over-reliant on the same set of activities with which I feel most confident (see also Wrench 2016; Wrench and Naylor 2013). So as well as pulling together my own practice knowledge, I have also researched the relevant literature to adapt ideas found in other publications or articles for assessment purposes. Where this is the case, I direct you to further reading.

In this book you'll find a wide range of direct work activities that are simply categorised and themed to enable you to quickly and easily identify exercises that are suitable when working individually or with family groups, at various stages in an assessment process and in diverse contexts. The plan is that you will be able to dip in and out of the book as you see fit. This might be for a one-off home visit, a core assessment or to ascertain the wishes and feelings of a young person about a range of issues, perhaps for a review, for a child protection conference, during care proceedings or for a family group conference. Many activities are applicable across a range of social care, health, education and therapy settings. You will then be able to work with children, young people and their families in more meaningful ways that illuminate their lived experiences, avoiding what Ferguson (2016) describes as children becoming 'invisible' in safeguarding practices.

Each exercise is simply formatted, outlining the materials you will need, together with the process and aims of the exercise, so that you and the child or family member can be clear what you are working on together. I have also added a 'Handy hints' section at the end of each activity to share my experiences of what has worked well for me and potential pitfalls to look out for. Where appropriate, I also offer ideas for extension activities or alternative applications of the exercise, but also encourage you to weave the techniques into your existing practice, using your own skills, knowledge and experience to develop the tools to meet the needs of children and their families you work with.

Above all, I encourage you to be creative and to use yourself in the work, whilst holding in mind the aims and objectives of the assessment. You need to believe in the activities you are bringing to this work if you want to instil confidence and belief in the child and the family. You must always consider the individual's needs and his developmental age and stage to tailor the activity accordingly, whether you're working with children or adult family members. Some exercises can be completed in 30 minutes or less, while others may take a couple of sessions. I offer a range of ideas in each area of the work, so you can always have a 'Plan B'. Although assessments are usually being conducted within tight time frames, you should always be respectful of the time the individual needs, knowing that strong feelings and difficult memories may be triggered by your work. As Treisman writes, 'the tools should be implemented with intentionality, care, thought, reflection, and caution' (Treisman 2017, p.25).

Finally, a few thoughts about the context to your direct work in assessments. In your preparation, always consider how you will describe your role, the purpose of the assessment and how the information that is gathered will be shared with others. Informed consent is critical.

You will need to be confident in your knowledge of normative child development[3] and the impact of complex developmental trauma on children to do so competently. 'Choosing the right words to explain their job should be tailored to each child and job and how much they already know about the practitioner and the work they do' (Howes, p.127 cited in Horwath 2010). Howes also invites practitioners to take account of considerations of family culture and ethnicity from the child's perspective and what you know of him. You will need to consider the child's perception of you as an individual and professional and what this might represent.

Be mindful of the belief systems and values of the child's culture, and how this could conflict or agree with your own core values and beliefs. Think about the structures and decision making in the child's close and extended family network and the child's place within this: Does he have a voice? What are the traditional solutions to problems in this system? Are sex and gender roles clearly defined? Consider the potential impact of moving to live in the UK if family members are first- or second-generation immigrants. There may also be racial or cultural pressures that could impact on the child if he talks to you.

Think too about the timing of the session, as there are practical issues to hold in mind that will impact on engagement, especially for children. Avoid meal times or the run-up to mealtimes, when children are likely to be more preoccupied with a rumbling tummy than interested in talking to you. They are also more likely to lose

---

3   There is a good chapter entitled 'The Developmental Needs of Children: Implications for Assessment' by Ward and Glaser in Horwath (2010) pp.160–173.

concentration. If you are seeing children during the school day make sure you check what they will be missing to meet with you. For example, will the session coincide with playtime, a favourite lesson or special treat like Golden Time? By scheduling the session more sensitively you reduce the risk of a child refusing to see you or rushing through to get the meeting over with as soon as possible.

Think about the location of the session, as challenges can arise here too. For example, make sure the child is comfortable with you coming into school as he may not want to be singled out as different from his peers. Ensure you support the child or young person with a 'cover story' if needed to explain where he has been during the session with you. If you are doing the work in the family home, think about the practicalities of keeping the child in the room and avoiding distractions. Also consider how 'free' the child will be to speak. Will it feel like a safe space? Will you be uninterrupted so there is a sense of privacy? Can you meet in the same room again?

Key characteristics of a sound analytical assessment

Assessment is a process, whereby analysis and reflection are taking place at every stage. We will never reach a point where we know everything there is to know, but we can weigh up what we learn throughout the process to inform our assessment and ultimately the outcome. This book will support you in gathering information about children and families and their circumstances; if the information spine and interpretation of what we have gathered is not robust enough, the synthesis and analysis of this data, which allows us to evaluate what we know and draw conclusions from it, will be inherently flawed. There needs to be a logical thread throughout the information spine, which will then support decision making, planning and intervention.

This book does not have analysis and critical thinking in assessment as its primary focus (see Dalzell and Sawyer 2016, and Brown and Turney 2014), as my emphasis is on the quality of the information available to analyse, think critically about, and use for planning and, where necessary, intervention. I am also mindful that local authorities and third sector organisations are using different models to enhance their assessment processes, such as *Signs of Safety* (Turnell and Edwards 1999) and *A Stepwise Model of Assessment* (Raynes 2003), so my focus is on active engagement with children and their families, as this should be at the heart of all assessment frameworks and good practice, irrespective of the model being used. I would also suggest that building working relationships and engagement are central to ensuring fair assessment processes and outcomes. Even the best evidenced toolkits and procedures are no replacement for professional judgement, sound, consistent practice and a relational focus.

Nonetheless to set the context, it does feel relevant to outline the core principles of good, evidence-informed assessment processes. Research in Practice describe evidence-informed practice (EIP) as a way of working where decisions about how to meet service user needs are based on an understanding of three areas:

- the best available research evidence about what works

- practice experience and expertise which we amass through our working lives, constantly building up a reservoir of evidence

- views of service users – about their expectations, preferences, impact of the difficulties they are facing and of our involvement.

(adapted from Leech 2014)

In undertaking assessments of vulnerable children and their families we must ensure these three domains are considered when we are testing out hypotheses to try to make sense of the complexities of family life. This should then lead us to sound, evidence-informed judgements and ultimately decisions and outcomes. Within this, of course, we must use analytical skills and critical thinking to 'show our workings out' or our reasoning. We need to demonstrate that we have sound reasons for what we think, do and recommend. We should be critically evaluating our personal beliefs and actions throughout to ensure they are not unhelpfully impacting outcomes for families.

If we can hold an open-minded stance, this supports us to think about different ways of understanding the information before us, before we commit ourselves to a fixed perspective. I find it useful to think of the scales of balance – on the one hand X but on the other hand Y. In every scenario, consider how you might play devil's advocate and look for alternative understandings or explanations. What can research evidence add to the balance? What does your past practice experience mean for your understanding of this child or family's situation? What does your intuition (your 'gut feeling') tell you – be alert to your own physiological responses, drawing on your life experience, as well as your knowledge of theory and research.

The Five Anchor Principles (Brown and Turney 2014) provide a simple framework to help with decision making in complex situations and can be used alongside standard assessment tools or models within your organisation.

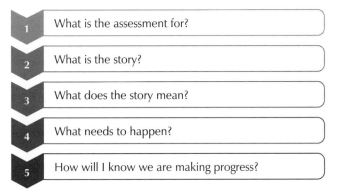

Figure i.2 The Five Anchor Principles
(adapted from Brown and Turney 2014)

Let's look at these five principles briefly.

What is the assessment for?

If you are clear about the purpose of the assessment, it's so much easier to identify the key issues and plan the assessment process. This is how you will begin to collate key information and knowledge that is pertinent to the child or family. What do you need to know? Who do you need to see? What do you need to read? What direct work or other assessment tools might you need to use? What research is relevant to inform your practice?

What is the story?

You need to decide what information is relevant that can be connected into a coherent narrative. Condense the facts of the story by identifying no more than eight key elements. It is impossible to exercise sound judgement unless there is a clarity of task and content, although the challenge is that in complex families both can change rapidly and often seem unclear.

What does the story mean?

It is only by extracting the meaning from the information spine (or the facts gathered) that you can critically analyse the situation. This is where you would think about theories that inform your understanding of the story. This might be attachment or trauma, change cycles or theories of loss and grief, for example. They help you look at the information and decide 'and so what?'

What needs to happen?

When you have made meaning from the story you will be able to ascertain what this says about the needs of the child and family, and from this will come your plan. You will find it much easier following these principles to be specific about how proposed actions will connect with identified needs. This is the 'now what' of the process and shouldn't be just a list of referrals to other agencies. The child and family should be actively involved in the formulation of any plans, ensuring you follow the SMART rules.

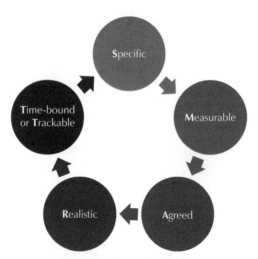

Figure i.3 SMART rules

You will need to agree realistic outcomes within this that you can use to effectively measure progress for the child and family. Decide together which outcomes to prioritise; agree who will work with the family towards goal achievement; consider whether multiple plans can run effectively alongside each other; identify any smaller goals that are more easily achievable to begin to build on family successes and motivate further change; determine when outcomes should be reviewed. To work effectively with vulnerable children and their families, it is vital that outcomes are child-focused, and this might require some negotiation skills, where there may be a conflict between parent/caregiver and practitioner goals or child's goals. Think about how the child would like his daily lived experience to look. What would need to change and what would this look like? Are aspects of his lived experience currently increasing the risk of harm or acting as protective factors?

How will we know we are making progress?

This is much more straightforward when you have agreed clear, intended outcomes with children and families and have been consistent about measures of progress. It is easier to measure 'hard outcomes' (such as improved school attendance, or completing a parenting programme) than 'soft outcomes', which measure changes in behaviour or confidence and are often more subjectively measured by asking for the opinions of others. They can include improved self-esteem or resilience or personal development. Have you been clear and explicit about what you want to achieve for this child and family as well as stating the implications of failure to make the necessary changes?

Then consider each outcome individually. If it hasn't been achieved, you will need to explore why not. Was there a flaw in your analysis? Were you testing out a hypothesis that has now been disproved? Has new information come to light, which wasn't given sufficient weight in your planning? Have you been unable to access an appropriate service to meet an identified need?

You will need a contingency plan in case little or no progress is made. And remember that if you as a practitioner are under extreme time pressure or too exhausted, under-resourced or overwhelmed to meaningfully engage with vulnerable families, it is so much easier for parents/caregivers to resist change, in some cases remaining disengaged with minimal challenge or indeed support. You are a valuable resource; by building relationships with children and families you will be able to enable identification of hopes and dreams, build resilience and confidence, and support families to resolve difficulties and dilemmas.

Challenges and barriers to successful assessment

In practice it can be a challenge to maintain focus on the child's needs, because of the necessity of building effective relationships with his parents/caregivers; adult cooperation is essential if the assessment process is to be useful. However, the reality of this work is that some children and families are harder to reach. We cannot talk about assessments without thinking about the impact of child or parent/caregiver resistance and *disguised compliance*, a somewhat divisive term first coined in 1988 in an inquiry into child deaths (Reder, Duncan and Gray 1988) and alluded to in many Serious Case Reviews (SCRs) where there have been concerns about the roles of involved agencies or professionals following the death or serious injury of a child. It is defined by the NSPCC (2014) thus: 'Disguised compliance involves parents giving the appearance of co-operating with child welfare agencies to avoid raising suspicions and allay concerns.' Practitioners can be met at times with outright hostility and at others by adults who seem to be working with us, but for diverse reasons aren't willing or able to make positive changes.

As part of the learning from SCRs, the NSPCC (2014) published a list of risk factors and lessons for practice in relation to families where disguised compliance had been considered a factor. They found disguised compliance resulted in practitioners missing opportunities to intervene. Concerns were not always given enough weight and so cases drifted. Professionals too easily accepted parents'/caregivers' stories without verification of the evidence.

In other cases, disguised compliance led to a disproportionate focus on meeting the parents'/caregivers' needs; the focus shifted too far away from the child. Practitioners became so focused on engaging the resistant adults that the need to achieve safer outcomes for children was sidelined. Of course, we know in safeguarding children that the adults very often have significant unmet needs of their own – typically a combination of mental health needs, substance misuse and domestic abuse. When one or more of these factors is involved, the known risks to children increase and professionals can become drawn into addressing the parental needs, thereby losing sight of the child. It is important to establish the facts and gather evidence about what is occurring rather than always accepting the parent's or caregiver's presenting behaviour or assertions. We must be alert to the dangers of becoming overconfident in a parent's/carer's capacity. 'By focusing on outcomes rather than processes professionals can keep the focus of their work on the child' (NSPCC 2014).

The issue of disguised compliance is a complex one and it's not surprising that at times it is hard to spot. Nicolas (2015) talks about families who promise to attend or work with services but then don't, or who engage with one service but not with others. She also notes that in many SCRs where parents/carers focused their energy on exemplary engagement with one agency (e.g. health or family support services) this deflected attention away from the fact that they were not working with other professionals. She highlights that:

> attendance is not the same as engagement. There are some families who know professionals put great stock on them attending meetings, parenting courses etc. and so they attend. The example I always give when I am delivering training is that delegates may be there on a three-line whip. They do not want to be there, they do not think they need to be there, they have far too much to do but they have been told they have to attend...the fact that they can tick the box and collect their certificate of attendance does not mean they have engaged with the subject matter, or taken anything in, or learned anything... As always, the evidence as to whether a parent/carer has engaged, as opposed to just attended, will be seen in whether they make any changes and whether the outcomes for the child start to improve. (Nicolas 2015)

Engagement with the assessment necessitates effort and commitment from parents and caregivers *and* workers, both in terms of attitude and behaviour. Platt (2012) has adapted Ward *et al.*'s (2004) Multifactor Offender Readiness Model (MORM) and applied it to statutory safeguarding practice. I find this diagram a useful tool when working with parents and caregivers. You might also like to look at the similar framework developed by Horwath and Morrison (2001) for assessing parents' commitment to change.

We're aiming for the top right box: *walk the walk and talk the talk*, where both commitment and effort are high. Parents should feel like there is a respectful working alliance maintained between them and professionals in the system. They will be coming to appointments, open to discussing strengths and difficulties, making use of the support that is offered and committed to completing agreed tasks, which will mean they can begin to better meet their child's needs.

If you observe a parent who appears committed to the plan but seems to be making little effort to effect positive change, then you are working with someone who is simply *talking the talk*. This person is full of good intentions in meetings or on home visits, but something always gets in the way of action. Mindful of restorative practices, you need to avoid the temptation to dive in to rescue these parents, doing things *for* or *to* them rather than *with* them, even when they present as genuinely distressed by the situation and sincere about wanting to address the problems.

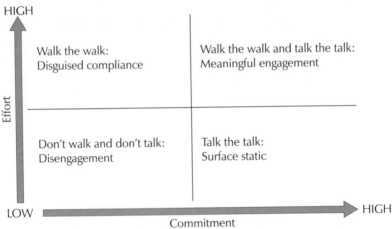

Figure i.4 Multifactor Offender Readiness Model (MORM)
(adapted from Horwath and Morrison 2001)

When parents look like they're working with you and are on board with a plan for assessment, but the child's daily life never looks any better, superficial cooperation could be masking antipathy or anger towards the practitioner or the agency. This can often be seen more commonly in families who have worked with social care before and may not have had a positive experience. With parents you think are *walking the walk*, it is essential that you look beyond verbal reports of change to find evidence of tangible differences that a child's quality of life or emotional wellbeing is improving.

Finally, parents who are *neither walking the walk nor talking the talk* are the parents we have not yet managed to engage. These parents/ caregivers have not opted in to change, and there may be many reasons for this. They may not have understood the concerns, or they may be so consumed or overwhelmed by their own difficulties (e.g. mental health, or drug or alcohol use) that they are unable to look beyond them to attend to the needs of their child. You will observe both fight and flight responses in these contexts. Ferguson and Norton (2011) talk about *flight behaviours* in parents who frequently move to a new house or out of area, who don't keep appointments or who limit access to the child or to what the practitioner sees or hears on home visits. You may also recognise the more common forms of disengagement which are *fight behaviours*: verbal and physical assaults on workers; vehement or aggressive refutation of the concerns; trying to threaten or intimidate, perhaps by threatening to make complaints or take legal action.

So, what works? How do you work effectively with resistance?

To confront these challenges effectively, practitioners need to sustain a position of 'healthy scepticism' and 'respectful uncertainly' when working with families (NSPCC 2015). It is never sufficient to simply record that the family has not engaged or only superficially engaged with the assessment. You need to consider the drivers for this. Why is this person avoidant? Why is he ambivalent? Why is he hostile? You will need to try to understand that resistance is functional; to some degree or another it will be linked with the relationship between you as the practitioner and the service user. This is helpful information; although as a practitioner you can be a factor in *creating* the resistance, so can you use yourself as a tool for *minimising* resistance. Ask yourself, 'What is getting in the way of me engaging this child or family?' rather than surmising, 'This child or family will not engage.' Have you, for example, missed anything critical in relation to gender, race, faith, ethnicity, physical or learning disability that is impacting on engagement?

Forrester *et al.* (2008) studied taped interviews between social workers and actors playing the part of parents and found that the factor most influential to a positive client response was empathy. This is not the same as over-identification with a client's experience or minimising the concerns. It is about validation of the feelings, allowing space for reflection, and, even when the information shared is difficult or problematic, considering 'and what else?'. When you ask exception questions about when a problem might be less overwhelming, less frequent or even absent, you can often initiate the hopeful building blocks for change. Genuinely empathetic workers are more likely to enable clients to share information and typically meet less resistance than those who ask closed questions in a problem-saturated interview. Practitioners need to demonstrate that they too can *walk the walk and talk the talk* in partnership with the family. This means actioning their own tasks in the assessment or plan and working collaboratively alongside the parents/carers. Without an engaged, committed worker with them, even the most well-motivated parent will find it more of a challenge to make any plan work.

However unpalatable it sounds, there will always be a minority of parents/carers who will not do what is needed to keep their children safe and well. It is vital if you feel you may be working with such a family, that you have the time and space to reflect on what might be happening; to talk to colleagues about the situation who might be able to offer a different perspective or challenge your views or hypotheses. Here I will summarise Nicolas's (2015) top tips for working in this challenging context:

- **Stand back**. With the benefit of hindsight, the evidence of disguised compliance can be obvious, but when we're in it, it can be hard to see it.

- **Make use of inter-professional relationships**. Talk to each other; when you are in regular communication with other agencies, splits happen less in systems. The Working Together guidance (HM Government 2015, p.9) reminds us, 'no single professional can have a full picture of a child's needs and circumstances and, if children and families are to receive the right help at the right time, everyone has a role to play in identifying concerns, sharing information and taking prompt action'.

- **Ensure there is capacity to change**. Remember there are two components to having capacity to make the changes needed; motivation is of equal value to mental capacity. If either is missing you are unlikely to see sustained positive change. Do more asking parents/caregivers what needs to change (if anything) rather than telling families what needs to change. (For more information on change cycles and capacity to change, see Chapter 9.)

- **Think about the use of written agreements very carefully**. Bear in mind that in *some* circumstances (domestic abuse being the prime example) parents will sign written agreements, for example agreeing not to allow the perpetrator of the violence into the family home, because they fear their children will be removed if they don't sign. What is the value of this agreement? To expect a parent to be able to keep to such an agreement, when s/he is in an altogether powerless position is not only unrealistic but also potentially places too much responsibility on the victim rather than the perpetrator of the abuse. Consent or agreement to work with a plan or failure to do so, may be indicative of coercion or fear rather than disguised compliance.

- **Use an integrated chronology**. This will pull together information from across all agencies – it is much easier to see the reality of what is happening, to focus on the facts and the evidence when you have the full picture, rather than relying solely on what the parents and caregivers are telling you about their work or relationships with other professionals.

- **Spend time with the child**. It is all too easy to focus on the adults' needs during a home visit or assessment session; by the end of the hour you may find you've spent 45–50 minutes speaking to the adults and 5–10 minutes with the child. Is this sufficient time to learn about and understand the child's needs and lived experiences? Don't only just listen to the parents/ caregivers. Listen to and be with the child to learn about his world.

- **Use evidence**. Wherever possible, make sure every decision and action you take is evidence-based. Don't take anything you see or hear at face value; always look for the evidence to back up what you are being told or what you think you have understood.

- **Identify the outcomes**. Clarity of outcomes will ensure you focus on meeting the needs of the child and on the evidence for change. Everyone should then be working to the same agreed goals, with clear timescales and transparent consequences if they are not achieved. You will need evidence of change, even if you could be persuaded otherwise by what parents or caregivers are telling you.

What distorts assessments?

There are additional factors that can influence the outcome of an assessment, most of which, as practitioners we absolutely need to take responsibility for ourselves. Horwath summarises many of these in her chapter 'Making Sense of Information, Planning Interventions and Reviewing Process' (2010, pp.71–87). We must keep an open mind throughout the assessment and not be unhelpfully bound to our original hypotheses, which are likely to be made upon incomplete or unsupported assumptions. Maintenance of accurate, contemporaneous recordings, written sensitively and respectfully, that avoid using jargon and abbreviations, are also key.

Subjective factors can also have a significant influence on the assessment process. Each practitioner brings his own personal and professional beliefs, feelings, values and life experiences to the workplace, within a specific organisational context. He may or may not be aware of the influence of these factors, but if these biases remain unconscious, they are more likely to distort the outcome. This could be in relation to his own attachment history, gender, or experiences of parenting or of being parented. 'This might also include a difficulty in empathising with another's world view, or feeling unsure about attitudes to parenting practices in other cultural groups' (Holland in Horwath 2010 p.121). It is then easier to become overdependent on knowledge of our past experiences of working with other families with 'similar' presenting difficulties.

Table i.1 Ways in which feelings and experiences can distort assessments

Subjective response	Impact on assessment
Over-optimism: A misguided positive belief in the carer's ability to meet the needs of the child. For example, 'Now that Dad knows what he has done wrong I'm sure the family will be OK. You know they are really nice people.'	This results in an overemphasis on assessing strengths and minimising concerns. The practitioner may accept the carer's perception that all is well without an evidence base.
Over-pessimism: A belief that the carer is unable to meet the needs of the child. For example, 'She's a hopeless case, the child is best out of there.'	This can lead to an assessment that focuses on concerns and parenting deficits, ignoring or minimising any strengths.

Collusion: Choosing to believe what carers say despite evidence to the contrary. For example, 'Mum is trying so hard, she's a lovely person; she says she's learnt her lesson and I believe her.'	In these situations workers focus on the carers' perspective and do not seek evidence to confirm or refute these beliefs, either through the current assessment or by identifying past patterns of behaviour.
Fixed idea: Holding a specific idea about the nature of the case, often prejudging a situation. For example, 'I know the problem is Dad's drinking; why bother with an assessment, it will just confirm this.'	The fixed idea is often formed early on. Indeed it may be their first hypothesis and they stick to it. In these situations practitioners tend to gather information that confirms their ideas and they ignore information that contradicts this.
Overriding beliefs: Having a fixed idea about the needs of the family and ways in which they can be met. For example, 'If only we could clean the house out the neglect would cease.'	In these situations practitioners make an early decision about appropriate interventions and ignore information that may indicate that these are not appropriate. A common overriding belief is that the family will eventually be able to meet the needs of the child when there is no evidence to indicate this and the child should be placed out of home.
Ignoring difference: Treating all families as the same. For example, 'Another dirty, smelly family.'	The practitioner tends to categorise families and make judgements about them without considering differences. This can be particularly common when working with families from different ethnic and religious backgrounds.
Avoidance: Failing to ask difficult questions or challenging what the carer says. For example, 'I did not ask him about his drinking. I did not want to annoy him.'	This response is most likely to occur if the practitioner is intimidated by the carer. In this situation, selected information is gathered. This is likely to be non-controversial or positive and can mean that areas of concern are not explored.

Source: Horwath (2010), reproduced with permission

CHAPTER 1

BUILDING SAFETY INTO THE ASSESSMENT PROCESS

A Trauma-Informed Response

Although no two individuals, families or systems are the same, there are factors they may have in common, particularly when considering how to engage families in assessment processes in the context of traumatic events. This is the case whether they are impacted by developmental trauma as children (Van der Kolk 2005), acute, non-personal traumas like a car accident or a natural disaster, or chronic interpersonal stressors such as domestic abuse. The impact of layers of adversity will often go far beyond the capacity of the individual to process single or multiple traumatic events, depending on the context, development stage of the victim, their external resources and challenges and the 'type, source, chronicity, and impact' of the event (Blaustein and Kinniburg 2010, p.4). (Also see the impact of adverse childhood experiences in Chapter 3.)

Blaustein and Kinniburgh (2010) propose a three-part model for understanding child behaviour in the context of traumatic stress, which I feel is also useful in assessments when considering adult family members, particular parents and caregivers with a history of relational trauma in childhood. Part one of the model relates to systems of meaning and the assumption of danger. We all have frames of reference that help us to understand ourselves and the world around us that develop throughout childhood, initially through our relationships with primary caregivers. We add 'layers of nuance and complexity' (2010, p.22) to these frames of reference as we grow and experience life and make assumptions based on previous experiences, about ourselves and others as well as how we interpret events. Where individuals have experienced repeated stressors, complex relational trauma or have lived in environments characterised by danger, chaos and unpredictability, it is not uncommon for their belief systems to become very rigid. This becomes relevant for assessments where vulnerable children and their families might have a set of assumptions relating to relationships that could include:

- I cannot trust anyone, especially adults or people in authority.

- I am not safe.

- No one can help me.

- I am powerless.

- The world is a dangerous place.

- I am not a good person. I don't deserve care.

The second part of this model relates to safety-seeking behaviours. Where individuals have lived for prolonged periods surrounded by danger, their brains and bodies can become over-sensitive to perceived threats in their environment, even though objectively they might recognise that the danger is not real. When explaining this to children I use the analogy of a smoke alarm that is set off when you're just frying bacon; it's a false alarm, there is no real 'emergency'. Similarly, 'the human danger response does not require actual, physical danger in order to be activated; it merely requires the *perception* [original italics] of danger. Once your brain has labelled something as dangerous, regardless of "objective reality," your body will respond' (Blaustein and Kinniburgh 2010, p.27). Where children and families have experienced long-term or ongoing stressors, the range of incoming signals or triggers that could be labelled by their brains as threatening or dangerous is vast. Again, this is critical to understand when you are entering family life at a point of crisis to undertake an assessment, often with little history or information about the family's lived experiences. You may represent danger or threat.

The third part of the model relates to interference from developmental gaps due to inadequate or distressed early caregiving systems and the alternative adaptations children subsequently make. Where children have experienced relational or developmental trauma

– or where their parents have had these experiences themselves as children – it is not uncommon to see core difficulties in the capacity to self-regulate, together with a real struggle to maintain a comfortable state of arousal within what is known as the 'window of tolerance', a term originally coined by Dan Siegel (1999). This is the zone of arousal in which we best function; we are emotionally regulated, we can self-soothe, we can think and speak.

Survivors of complex trauma can experience triggers in the here and now that remind the body and the brain of the past, thereby activating the nervous system into believing that it is under attack again, moving out of the window of tolerance into hyper- or hypo-aroused states. Until practitioners help vulnerable children and their caregivers to function within the window of tolerance, they will not readily be able to receive, process and integrate information and respond to the demands of everyday life without great difficulty. Their ability to contribute meaningfully to the assessment process will also be compromised.

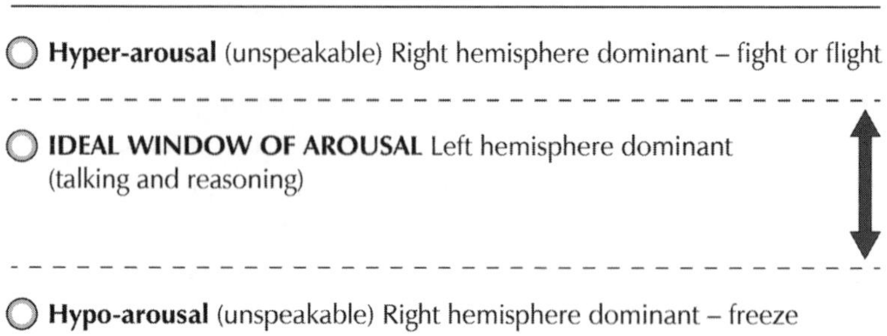

○ **Hyper-arousal** (unspeakable) Right hemisphere dominant – fight or flight

○ **IDEAL WINDOW OF AROUSAL** Left hemisphere dominant
(talking and reasoning)

○ **Hypo-arousal** (unspeakable) Right hemisphere dominant – freeze

Figure 1.1 The window of tolerance

Everyone's window of tolerance/arousal is different and can be impacted by their environment; in general terms, individuals are better able to remain within the window when they feel supported and safe. A narrowed window of tolerance can be the result of earlier traumatic experiences and can lead to a belief that the world is unsafe. Individuals can learn how to widen their unique window of tolerance, often using grounding or mindfulness techniques to help them stay present in the moment.

Trauma responses

When we perceive a threat, the body, instructed by the brain, automatically responds and prepares to deal with the apparent danger. The brain initiates a release of chemicals that provide our bodies with the energy we need to cope with the threat. The response occurs in milliseconds; our arousal level increases, we experience a shift in sensory perception, and non-essential functions like digestion shut down. Higher cognitive processes like impulse control, logic and planning can also go offline at these times.

How we respond when faced with a perceived threat is somewhat dependent upon the situation: simply put this is known as *fight, flight or freeze* (Levine 1997). Running away to escape the threat might be an option if you are a faster runner than the person or thing causing the emergency, or if there is someone or somewhere safe to run to. This often offers our best chance of survival (*flight*). Screaming or yelling are also good options to let people around you know there is a problem, but only if you are near someone who can hear you and be helpful, and not out on a deserted country lane. If you were being attacked, you may choose to try to fight back, but ultimately the success of any strategy is dependent upon the power differential between the individual and potential source of danger (*fight*). The disabling freeze response is often the option utilised by children, as their developmental capacity to protect themselves is so limited; it is the defence we use when we can neither defeat nor run from the threat (*freeze*). Children often use avoidant or psychological fleeing mechanisms such as dissociation. Like the alarm response, the intensity of dissociation varies according to intensity, frequency and duration of the stressor.

The behaviours we see in children and their caregivers when they perceive danger can vary. We know that although we may be unaware of it, some situations in the here and now can remind us of previous traumas; never fully discharged, the original fear or panic linked with the memory of the event compels us to act as if it were happening all over again. This can be thought of as an over-active alarm system; it cannot distinguish between false alarms and actual danger. Common triggers for traumatised children include:

- changes of plan or unpredictability

- transitions

- feeling a loss of control

- feeling rejected or vulnerable

- limit setting or confrontation

- feeling lonely

- sensory overload.

Sometimes it's impossible to identify the trauma trigger; the danger response may result from an individual living in a state of high stress, which serves as an unconscious reminder of the stress of the initial trauma. Remember also that threat may come from an internal source, such as physical pain or discomfort, or from an external source, such as a social worker. You may well be interpreted as a threat when undertaking assessments and need to be alert to the signs that someone is feeling unsafe with you.

Fear dramatically alters thinking, feeling and behaviour, so you need to be aware of what these arousal states might look like during your assessment. Remember also that individuals experiencing the same traumatic event (e.g. siblings present during a domestic abuse incident) can develop different adaptive styles to cope with stressors. Tables 1.1 and 1.2 give suggestions of common fight, flight, freeze responses in adults and children, and although these are by no means exhaustive lists, they will support you in recognising possible signs that a child or adult is not feeling safe.

Table 1.1 Trauma responses in adults

Fight	Freeze	Flight
Crying	Feeling stuck in some part of the body	Restless legs/numb legs
Hands in fists, desire to punch/rip	Feeling cold/frozen, numb, pale skin	Anxiety/shallow breathing
Tight jaw, grinding teeth, snarl	Stiffness or heaviness	Big or darting eyes
Desire to kick, stamp, smash with feet	Holding breath or restricted breathing	Leg/foot movement
Suicidal feelings/self-harm	Heart pounding or sense of dread	Restlessness, tension, feeling trapped
Rage/anger	Orientation to threat	Excessive exercise
Knotted stomach	Decreased heart rate (though can sometimes increase)	Running from one activity to the next

Source: adapted from www.trauma-recovery.ca/impact-effects-of-trauma/
fight-flight-freeze-responses

In children you may observe different responses. Look for moments when the intensity of the child's response doesn't match the context. Does his response or behaviour confuse you or seem hard to explain? If so, ask yourself could this be his faulty 'smoke alarm'?

Table 1.2 Trauma responses in children

Fight	Flight	Freeze
Oppositional behaviour	Withdrawal	Stilling
Verbal/physical aggression	Escaping	Watchfulness
Hyperactivity/bouncing off walls/silliness	Running away	Daydreaming or looking dazed
Testing boundaries	Avoidance – sit alone in class	Over-compliance or denial of needs
Trouble concentrating	Self-isolation – stay in bedroom, not doing activities	Shutting down emotionally/ constricted emotional expression

Source: adapted from Blaustein and Kinniburgh (2010, p.27)

There are also two further Fs to add to the well-documented 3Fs. I was introduced to them by Zoe Lodrick (2007), citing Ogden and Minton (2000) and Porges (1995, 2004). These are *friend* and *flop*. *Friend* is the most primitive, earliest response to danger, otherwise known as the social engagement system. Lodrick (2007) talks about the immobile infant, who can only cry to bring a caregiver close to provide relief. As children grow, they become able to move towards a source of safety to seek protection and with the acquisition of language they also have the option to try to negotiate, bribe or plead their way out of danger.

The fifth F is *flop*, the most likely response if all other strategies have failed; it usually follows freeze – the strategy used when friend, fight or flight have been unsuccessful. The body shifts from a state of muscular tension to a floppy state. Lodrick (2007, p.6) describes how the 'survival purpose of flop is evident: if "impact" is going to occur the likelihood of surviving it will be increased if the body yields, and psychologically in the short term at least, the situation will be more bearable if the higher brain functions are "offline."' Flop is commonly utilised in incidents of sexual assault or physical abuse.

Practical strategies to build safety into assessments

For traumatised individuals to begin to think, engage with the world, learn and explore, the most significant factor is to begin to believe they are safe and can trust. To begin to create a sense of safety for the child and family in your assessment work, your priority must be to convey that you are safe, consistent, emotionally available and dependable if any trust is to develop. Be clear from the beginning about the focus of the assessment and of each session, so there are no surprises. Of course, sometimes you may need to go off course or change the plan mid-session, but your structure should still be maintained with a clear beginning, middle and end. If the beginning and ending of your session or visit remain consistent throughout the assessment, this helps promotes a feeling of safety and predictability. Perhaps you will begin with some quick warm-up activities or a check-in and end with the ritual of a story or a song.

If you become aware that a child is in a trauma state (hyper- or hypo-aroused), you will need to offer some modulation activity to soothe his sensory system. In fact, such activities can be useful at the start and end of any session. A child with high energy will need different options to a child who is withdrawn. The 'fizzy' child may need to expend energy, so movement can be helpful. You could suggest a bounce on the trampoline outside in the garden or try counting how many star jumps he can do in a minute. Go for a fast, marching walk outdoors or play a game of push me over, pull me up with a younger child. A more withdrawn child will certainly benefit from activities that connect you, like throwing a ball to each other or blowing a feather across a cushion and back. All these sorts of activities activate the brain stem and can support improved regulation. Base your activity on where the child's energy level is at.

If you notice children beginning to dysregulate or see evidence of high arousal, it can help to have a little bag or box filled with options for sensory soothing. You can include something for the child to suck like a lolly or juice/water bottle or to chew like a toffee. It could be a sensory toy like a tangle or fidget cube to occupy little hands and ease anxiety. Gently blowing bubbles or simple, child-friendly breathing exercises are also soothing activities to do together (see calm box in Chapter 2).

If the context is appropriate (see in the Introduction re: domestic violence and disguised compliance), I would strongly recommend that you first create a *working agreement* together. For an adult this is traditionally a signed written contract, but there is no reason why you shouldn't use a creative approach to the working agreement with adults in appropriate situations, as well as children and young people. The most important factor is the clarity of information shared, and coming to an agreement about how you'll work together moving forward; transparency of aims and goals.

You'll only need basic resources for this such as drawing paper and pens. Other collage materials, such as coloured paper, glue, stickers and tissue paper squares, are nice to have but not essential. The working agreement becomes a document that sets the ground rules for your sessions with the child and his family. When working with vulnerable groups, you must be predictable; there is safety built into sameness. However, there are no limits to how creative you can be in this task, and I usually try to incorporate some of the child's interests within the image. For example, you could use a sporting theme, animals or a favourite TV programme, which aids engagement by capturing the child's interest. Coming prepared with images you know the child is more likely to connect with also gives a strong message of his having been held in mind by you.

The child might like to contribute his own ideas about the work, such as playing a quick game at the beginning of the assessment sessions or agreeing a way of letting you know when he needs a break. This is especially important for children or young people who have already been victimised and might feel anxious about not being able to control the process; but don't disregard this as an important factor for traumatised adults too. It can be reassuring to be asked: 'How will you let me know if you need a break?' or 'How will you tell me if you feel unsafe or can't talk about something just now?'

The agreement should include key information about what to expect from the assessment process, including practical arrangements such as where and when you will meet and how many sessions you will have together and for how long. This is also the time to talk about confidentiality and the limitations of information boundaries. You will need to explain with whom the information you gather will be shared and where it will be recorded. Where you are undertaking assessments alongside a criminal investigation, also be mindful of requirements for witnesses as part of any criminal proceedings and apply the relevant guidance, which can be accessed at www.cps.gov.uk.

When working with children or family groups, I also suggest you use some brief 'getting to know you' activities and games to facilitate engagement and begin to build trust in a more child-centred way. If you find an activity, game or story the child likes, bring it with you every time. Consistency like this can be a significant tangible ritual; the same applies to bringing the same selection of toys in your toolkit (see Chapter 2). Remember that children who have experienced relational trauma will have a belief that the world and others are unsafe, so building routines and rituals into your interactions can help decrease feelings of insecurity and vulnerability. You may need to pay attention to the child's need for control around your interactions. If you bring a structured activity of your choosing, it can be a good idea to factor in time for some free play or an activity of the child's choice.

Sharing positive or creative experiences with a child and his family is often a good way of breaking the ice and beginning to build relationships, but a simple game of hangman or noughts and crosses can work just as well. There are some great applications that can be played on an iPad or smartphone, which encourage more resistant young people to join you in a quick ice breaker game. Rose (2012) uses Jenga as a tool for introductions and relationship building in work with parents or caregivers and their children. He writes:

> As the process begins I am interested in how each person plays the game; whether the child plays to win, and whether the adult does the same. I am interested in alliances, support, encouragement and engagement, as well as the verbal cues; I am particularly keen to identify the nonverbal cues. (Rose 2012, p.103)

He goes on to consider a checklist to evaluate the communication and, for assessment purposes, it is useful to consider the following in relation to family members playing this or other games, or indeed, doing any creative activities together. How does the child and adult:

- assess risk?

- approach the task?

- cope with anticipation?

- manage with pressure and tension?

- encourage, engage and/or play strategically?

- offer support, advice and/or guidance to each other?

- react when successful?

- react when others are successful?

- show empathy?

- react to the possibility of failure?

- react to the failure?

(Rose 2012, p.104)

Exploration of children's and the family's lives through play or sharing enjoyment in a task can be a useful intervention in itself, as well as helping to create the kind of environment where they will feel enabled and safe enough to explore potentially more difficult issues with you during the assessment process. Games are a great way to begin to understand how individuals have learnt to adapt to their world and to respond to the environment around them. What you will observe is the surface behaviour, but underneath this behaviour – the trouble concentrating, the sibling rivalry, the self-reliance or the rigid need to control – 'is the brain doing its best to ensure survival by sacrificing some tasks for the sake of others' (Blaustein and Kinniburgh 2010, p.3). This resonates with the iceberg model from the work on culture by Selfridge and Sokolik (1975). Behaviour is visible to others above the surface of the ocean, but the things that drive that behaviour (our thoughts, beliefs and values) are hidden below the surface, unseen by others. To understand (and change) behaviour, we must be alert to what is below the surface. In many vulnerable families, behaviour that might be labelled or pathologised as abnormal, may well be alternatively understood as signs of survival or having learned to adapt to living in a difficult environment.

Other ideas for breaking the ice and relationship building include:

- **A getting-to-know-you collage**. Use collage materials including photographs, Google images, magazines and craft materials. You could suggest co-creating a shared image, model or collage of 'safe' things about yourselves. A visually impaired child could make a collage using tactile connections with safety. This can be done with an individual child, sibling or family group.

- **All-about-me badge**. Make a badge to share information about each other. If working with a family or sibling group, this is a simple task everyone can join in. Have a circle of paper that you divide into sections – for example, something I like to do, something I am good at, something I need help with or that I'd like to work on, something or someone that is special to me, the name of a good friend, something that worries me.

Figure 1.2 All-about-me badge

You could also make a Me Tree displaying the child's or family's interests, likes and dislikes on branches and leaves (Lippett 1990).

- **All About Me**. The All About Me game produced by Barnardo's (www.barnardos.org.uk/resources) follows the familiar format of a colourful board game, with dice and counters to take children and families on a path of discovery through feelings and experiences, some of which they may find difficult to express or deal with. There is a selection of cards that you can tailor to the needs of the child or family. Some are innocuous, but others can help you get to the heart of more tricky issues in family life.

- **The T-Shirt**

Figure 1.3 T-shirt templates

Have T-shirt templates like the ones above or simply draw a T-shirt and ask the person to draw an image or write a message on the T-shirt under these three headings:

- how I believe people see me or would describe me

- what people would see if they really knew me (What am I trying to hide?)

- how I would like to be seen or thought of by others.

If you're feeling especially creative you could bring old T-shirts and fabric paints and ask the family to make 'real' shirts.

CHAPTER 2

COMMUNICATION AND CREATIVITY

We have already begun to explore the importance of relationships in the assessment process and have considered the impact of relational trauma on our capacity to engage with others, particularly at times of stress. Communication skills are also crucial to success in assessments, so it is important to acknowledge the vast range of communication options open to us, especially taking into account what we understand about the impact of trauma on functioning. The way we approach and respond to communication with children, young people and their parents/carers will directly influence the outcome of that interaction. It will also determine whether we support emotional wellbeing or risk dysregulating already traumatised individuals further.

Communication 'includes conveying, sharing, exchanging, transmitting, broadcasting and receiving information, ideas and feelings between people. In its simplest form, communication can be defined as the process of transmitting information from one person to another' (Dunhill 2009, p.19). It is vital that we engage in the right kind of communication at the right time to support vulnerable children and their families to work with us. If we achieve this, we can ensure that people are more able to express their views, to share their experiences and needs, and to actively contribute to the assessment. We are then more able to work *with* and *alongside* children and families rather than doing *to* and *for* them (Wachtel 2005). This absolutely fits with working restoratively to build and maintain healthy relationships, resolve difficulties and repair harm where there has been conflict; we must focus on building relationships that create change, in the knowledge that this approach will at times require high challenge as well as high support as seen in the Social Discipline Window (Figure 2.1).

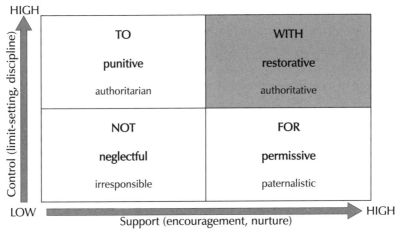

Figure 2.1 The Social Discipline Window
(adapted from Wachtel 2016)

First impressions are vital as we all rapidly appraise people we meet and form opinions of them. This is even more important when working with people who have experienced trauma. 'After trauma the world is experienced with a different central nervous system that has an altered perception of risk and safety. Porges coined the term "neuroception" to describe the capacity to evaluate relative danger and safety in one's environment.' People with faulty neuroception have their survival mechanism working against them; they quickly move to a position of fight or flight. They have lost the capacity to experience safety, relaxation and reciprocity (Van der Kolk 2014) and are likely to misread our intentions. Trauma can then be expressed not only as fight or flight, but as shutting down and not being able to engage in the moment. This clearly has significant implications in assessments (see also Chapter 1).

In the context of assessments, practitioners may also have already begun to make judgements about a child or family member based on referral or historic information before the first meeting. Those individuals will undoubtedly also have views and expectations of us as workers, based on their previous experiences, the media, or the understandings friends and family have of social care. Koprowska (2008, p.53) distils her advice in terms of constructive, empowering engagement into four key principles: 'be clear, concise, comprehensive and courteous'. To be *clear* we need to use 'simple, direct language, free from jargon and pompous phraseology'. To be *concise*, we should be adequately prepared for the assessment session, aware of the key issues and able to 'communicate them succinctly'. To be *comprehensive* we need to keep all the key issues at the forefront of our minds and be alert to information that could side line or make us feel uncomfortable. Finally, to relate in a *courteous* manner, Koprowska insists we need to be aware of 'much more than just good manners'. She refers also to core social work values: 'our respect for individuals and their uniqueness, and our commitment to anti-discriminatory and anti-racist practices and hence our respect for diversity'.

Speech and language

Communication using speech and language allows us to fulfil multiple functions. We can express our needs and know what others are asking of us. We can exchange or share information about our lives and understand when others tell us what they think is happening. We can share information about things that cannot necessarily be observed or seen. We communicate to make and sustain relationships, to play and use our imaginations. It can be understood as fundamental to most activity and it is certainly crucial in assessments.

In any situation where we are talking and listening to children, various factors will impact effective communication, so we must be mindful of children's language ability and typical language acquisition. Notice how the child talks in everyday terms, so you can adjust your language accordingly. Make it a habit to use basic words and clear sentences and to avoid jargon. In terms of direct engagement with young children, a helpful general guide is to talk to the child in sentences that are no more than one word longer than the sentences the child is producing himself. Koprowska (2008) suggests a child may use about 50 words by 16–22 months, but will understand four times as many. Typically, by 18–24 months, two-word phrases occur, swiftly followed by three-word phrases. Children of three years will understand *what*, *where* and *who* questions, whilst by five, they start to be able to answer *when* questions competently. Before then, understanding of abstract concepts such as yesterday, tomorrow or soon is really limited.

When very young children are present during discussions with their caregivers, remember that they usually know what words mean, and understand much of what is being said around them, even if they can't yet articulate any recognisable words themselves (DfES 2005). Also consider that very young children (under-threes) are unlikely to communicate confidently with an adult stranger unless they have a trusted parent or carer close by or are in a familiar setting like home or nursery. Similarly, a pre-school child would typically only manage to tolerate separation from his primary caregiver for a short period before becoming upset. Remember that all children can at times be highly selective about where, when and how they use language.

Good tips for communicating with younger children with developing language include:

- working to hold their attention; frequent use of the child's name, high pitch and exaggerated tone

- careful use of vocabulary in brief, simple sentences

- more repetition than usual

- greater use of questions, prompts, directions

- frequent expansion of the child's speech

- commentary on the child's activities.

If you observe a parent or caregiver adjusting his speech in this way (sometimes known as *motherese*), these characteristics are usually perceived as a good source of language learning for the child.

When we focus on gathering information verbally to inform our assessments, we are usually asking questions. They may be *closed* or *narrow questions*, which are designed to obtain facts and can often be answered with a 'yes' or a 'no'. These questions are usually easy to understand and allow you to offer alternatives as well as checking out facts. *Broad* or *open questions* are helpful when you want to explore or learn more about the person as they elicit explanations, ideas, suggestions or points of view. To help us to order the information or facts that emerge, it is useful to paraphrase and summarise; both these techniques allow us to check we have understood the facts and reflect our efforts to hear and accurately record what has been said. They create natural pauses, which can be particularly useful where service users have a lot to say. Summaries at the beginning and end of sessions can also ensure you agree on key points of discussion (Koprowska 2008).

Communication, involving an exchange of messages or meaning making, uses all the senses, although inevitably most people focus on speech and language as they are considered to convey the most complex meanings. However, Koprowska (2008, p.11) also refers to *paralanguage*: the other strands of communication like pitch, volume, speed and tone that convey the emotional content of a message. Non-verbal cues are estimated to be responsible for up to 80 per cent of what helps a client feel safe in therapy, (Glenn, Jaffe and Segal n.d.), so in your assessment sessions you also will need to be tuned in to the subtle cues you pick up from the child or family member, including eye contact, gesture, fidgeting, facial expression and posture.

Emotion is felt, seen and expressed in the body. Notice whether words and feelings are congruent during your assessment. Where they don't match, which do you believe – the words or the body language? Be aware also of what physical and emotional experiences you communicate back through your own non-verbal communication. People who have experienced relational and developmental trauma will be vigilant to potential signals of incoming threat; 'think carefully about body language, body positioning, tone of voice, facial expressions and how one is conveying verbally and non-verbally the qualities of containment, responsiveness, sensitivity, warmth, being genuine, being present and being caring' (Treisman 2017, p.30).

Writing about social work with disabled children living away from home, Marchant (2008, p.155) reminds us:

> Children communicate best – especially about things that matter deeply – without language: showing, gesturing, playing, drawing, smiling, laughing, crying, making sounds, being quiet, moving, keeping still, hurting themselves or others. Broadening our definition of what is communication would benefit all children.

Barriers to communication

There are diverse barriers to effective communication and being aware of them is part of becoming a conscious communicator. A child or family's competence in communication is not fixed and can be enhanced or diminished by the skill of the practitioner. The barriers include:

- **Environmental factors**. Sometimes the environment isn't conducive to certain kinds of communication. Perhaps there are too many distractions; TV, visitors, or younger children to care for. Perhaps the context is wrong for the kind of conversation you need to have. I know we sometimes lack good room availability to meet with young people, but we don't always have to take them to McDonalds. It's not the ideal setting for a conversation that should be confidential and could therefore be difficult for young people to manage. Perhaps a walk in the park might be more appropriate.

- **Preoccupation with our own lives or thoughts**. Sometimes, as we listen, our minds are busy planning how we might respond or what follow-up question to ask. Or we might be thinking about a personal issue that's on our mind: 'Will I finish this visit in time to pick up my child from day care before it closes?' When we do this, we are not fully present and risk missing much of what is being communicated. We may be hearing but not necessarily listening.

- **Personal judgements or biases**. As someone is speaking we may, in our own heads, be developing a running monologue on what we're hearing or seeing. 'Well, I don't believe that for a minute.' 'Why hasn't she picked the baby up – he's crying.' Judgements can quickly fill up our minds. We may have personal biases about what is being said, about the person himself, about the conditions in the home, about choices that person has made. These biases can get in the way of truly hearing the story.

- **Cultural factors**. Different cultures (and generations) have different ways of communicating, including the use of spoken word and body language. Without knowledge of cultural norms, we might be offended by communication; misunderstand or misinterpret the intentions of gestures and vice versa. We may not comprehend the language used (e.g. slang or dialect) and might feel too self-conscious to ask for clarification. Where an individual has a strong accent or where English isn't their first language, we may find ourselves tuning out, therefore losing some of what is being said.

- **How you feel about yourself on the day**. If, for example, you feel intimidated by the person you are communicating with or lack confidence for whatever reason, it can be hard for the conversation or activities you have introduced to flow. You tend to focus on yourself – whether you said the right thing, how you look, what the family thinks of you – rather than on listening to what is being said.

Creativity and communication

So, having concentrated initially on verbal communication and body language, we also need to consider the impact of creativity on communication and how this can facilitate expression when words alone cannot. Don't be fooled by the common stories we tell ourselves about why we cannot or should not work creatively with children and families, which include:

- **'I don't have time.'** The assessment session itself should take no longer when you are working creatively than a typical, more traditional home visit does. The time-consuming part is usually the planning of the activity. However, the exercises in this book are set out so simply and thematically that it should only take a couple of minutes to flick through and identify a couple of appropriate options before you leave the office. With a creative toolkit in your boot, you should be ready to go.

- **'I don't have any resources.'** Most of the activities I describe need few if any resources other than pens and paper, or can be easily homemade and then re-used at very little cost. When you're starting out, make charity shops and car boot sales your best friends and beg or borrow unwanted toys from friends and family. You'll be surprised how quickly you can build an effective toolkit.

- **'I'm not confident in working creatively.** I was rubbish at art at school.' Well then practise – on your colleagues, your children, nephews and nieces. Begin with an activity you feel more confident with and with a child who you think will be easier to engage. Your confidence will come with experience. Use magazines and Google images to help you make suitable resources or visual prompts. If you laminate them, they can be endlessly re-used.

When you resolve to work creatively, through art making or play for example, you begin a conversation. As soon as someone shares his artwork or plays with you, he invites you to join the conversation. Like any other form of conversation, some people find expressing themselves creatively confusing or intimidating, while others find it sets them at ease and facilitates communication. In assessment terms think of creativity as introducing another language, perhaps where words cannot be found or feelings and experiences are too difficult to articulate; this is particularly critical when exploring traumatic events, which are often encoded in sensory fragments: a smell, a sound, an image, a taste, a bodily sensation. In assessments when we are asking children and families to explore traumatic memories, it makes sense to 'work at a creative contextual, embodied, semantic, narrative and sensory level (e.g. visual, kinaesthetic, tactile, olfactory, affective and auditory), where children can engage all of their senses in a relational, safe, contained and connected way' (Treisman 2017, p.35).

Van der Kolk's research identified that when traumatised individuals experience a flashback to a traumatic event, Broca's area, one of the speech centres of the brain, goes offline, meaning it is impossible in that moment to put thoughts and feelings into words. Even years after a traumatic event:

> traumatized people often have enormous difficulty telling other people what happened to them. Their bodies re-experience terror, rage, and helplessness, as well as the impulse to fight or flee, but these feelings are almost impossible to articulate. Trauma by nature drives us to the edge of comprehension, cutting us off from language based on common experience or an imaginable past. (Van der Kolk, 2014, p.43)

Even where individuals do eventually find the words to talk about what happened to them, the narrative rarely captures, as Van der Kolk puts it, 'the inner truth of the experience'.

So, for example, if you are visiting a parent and child following a recent incident of domestic abuse, consider whether it's reasonable to expect him to have the capacity to *talk* to you coherently about what has just been endured? Traumatised individuals may literally not have the words to speak of their experiences. When the lower brain is over-activated and focused on survival, the capacity of an individual to perform higher functioning tasks like problem-solving, creating a coherent narrative account or making good judgements can be impaired. Therefore, accept that even in Section 47 child protection enquiries, where timescales are tight and risks are potentially high, the families you arrive to assess may find it incredibly difficult to answer your questions or to give hard facts about their own actions, thoughts or feelings.

By introducing creative approaches to the assessment process, you allow both for self-expression but also *meaning making* through specific activities. Children and families can be supported to visually express and record their experiences, perceptions, feelings and imagination. If we want to understand a child's internal world as well as his external reality, we need to attend to what is communicated non-verbally by offering child-centred, creative or play-based opportunities. Unless you have accessed formal therapeutic training (like play therapy or art psychotherapy), it is essential not to step outside of the boundaries of your skill and experience when working creatively with children and families. These are protected titles so you will not be offering play or art therapy, rather working with children using play and art techniques. There should be no expectation that practitioners using symbolic or creative means of communication should be operating at the level of a qualified therapist. Creative arts should instead 'be seen as bridges to open up communication with children who are finding it hard to express themselves and engage with others at a direct or verbal level' (Lefevre 2008a, p.130).

By its simplest definition art making is a form of non-verbal communication. For individuals who, for whatever reason, are unable to articulate their thoughts, feelings or experiences verbally, it is an alternative way of conveying or sharing what cannot be spoken about. For those who have experienced abuse or who may have been silenced by the perpetrator, it can be a way of 'telling' more safely. As a sensory approach, it also allows individuals to experience themselves and communicate on multiple levels: visual, tactile, kinaesthetic, etc. With a tangible end product, children and their parents can not only be *heard* but also be *seen*. Certain sensory aspects of art making also seem to help with regulation, calming both the mind and the body, which is crucial for maintaining traumatised individuals within the window of tolerance during assessment sessions. This is why this book focuses so heavily on creative techniques for engaging children and their families.

It can be scary or intimidating for children and their parents/caregivers to engage in assessments, especially when they know the stakes are high. Self-expression in a formal setting can also be especially challenging for young children, who might have a limited vocabulary, or for families where English is a second language; and yet, when offered art materials, what often emerges is a richer representation of the child's world than he might be able to articulate verbally or what might emerge when constricted by the worker's suggestions about what to draw.

It is important not to begin to try to interpret the symbolism in a child's artwork or to understand images as literal statements connected with lived experience. Comment neutrally on what you see and on how the child is using the materials, which helps you to stay connected. It is important that the child feels neither led, judged nor criticised so open questions are preferable. 'Can you tell me about your picture?' rather than 'Is that your house?' In this way you avoid constraining possible understandings or meanings of the image and you are likely to elicit maximum information. If children (or indeed adults) go off on a tangent, it can be useful to allow this to happen at least for a while, as you gain insight into their communication style and may hear useful information you might not have thought to ask about.

Tait and Wosu (2013) also have a technique they call Right/Wrong Stones, which is useful when children, for whatever reason, are unable to easily communicate, often in adolescence. These children either refuse to speak or give monosyllabic 'yes' or 'no' responses. Tait and Wosu use a wide-necked, transparent jar, together with a selection of polished stones or shells and a timer. The timer is set and the worker begins by making a statement about the child or young person. If the statement is true, the young person puts a stone in the jar, but if it is false, a stone is removed. After three minutes of rapid-fire statements, the timer will beep, the stones are counted and roles reversed. The winner is the person with the most stones left in the jar when the time is up.

Ideas for statements include:

- Your name is...

- You are a boy/girl.

- You go to X school.

- You are in year X.

- You live with X, Y and Z.

- You are a bit nervous about playing this game.

- You like playing on the Xbox.

- You are wearing earrings.

- You have a pet dog.

- You understand why we are meeting.

- You don't like football.

- You love street dance.

- You like that it's a windy day.

- You don't like that this room is freezing cold.

Make sure you include some safe statements that are not too personal and introduce the rule of the beep, which gives the child an escape route. If he doesn't wish to answer a question, he can just make a beeping sound. Also include some clearly incorrect statements and some that are a little bit silly. These can be a great way of breaking the ice and having a bit of fun but also help check whether the young person has understood the rules of the game.

Another simple technique is a modification of the message in the bottle, where the child is asked to say or write a message to send to another planet, which represents something he is happy or unhappy about in relation to family life, school, health, etc. The aim in the original school-based research was to allow potentially marginalised views to surface (Davies 2000).

Children often tend to be 'doers' rather than talkers, and so active methods of engagement can work much better. Young children are also naturally creative; it can be easier for them to draw a picture than to answer your questions directly. You can simply ask: 'Can you show me what that looks like?' Older adolescents can be more resistant and aware of whether they are 'any good at art' or not. I find this self-consciousness is often soothed by offering tactile objects to fiddle with, which can help them to relax and remain regulated. I have a 'calm box' with a selection of fiddle toys like Tangles, smooth stones, a beanbag and hand cream to choose from, which helps to calm their brains and bodies. This replicates the idea of the use of activities as something for the worker and young person to focus on that takes the awkwardness or intensity out of the interaction. It can successfully diffuse tension.

Figure 2.2 A calm box

Similarly, many children and young people will benefit from a drink and snack (nurture) before you start your session. It's hard to concentrate when you're hungry, and for some children the actions of sucking (a toffee sweet, a juice bottle), crunching (a pretzel or carrot stick) or chewing (gum or a jelly sweet) can also soothe an over-aroused nervous system. There is also evidence that simple art activities can help to soothe the lower regions of a traumatised brain that remain on high alert, scanning instinctively for danger. The first step potentially in the assessment process is often exactly this: to allow service users to feel calmer and safer, which will support them to engage collaboratively in the assessment. Offering access to the creative arts is one way of achieving this. Trauma memories are, after all, sensory memories; people feel them in their bodies and react with their bodies. Creativity, as well as soothing the brain and the body, can also support movement towards understanding and self-expression.

Creating artwork can be experienced as a much less threatening way of expressing hostile or scary feelings or tackling subjects a person might be reluctant to talk about; the visual image can hold great power in externalising or giving form to difficult or messy emotions. Of course, it goes without saying that this approach doesn't suit every child and family; some children will express themselves wholly on the page whilst others need much more time and space or another medium before they can let you know about their lives.

Your creative toolkit

Most child and family workers will have felt-tip pens and paper in their bags to occupy children while they talk to the adults. However, when we work with what brings familiarity, this can be limiting; the more creative options and approaches you feel confident using the better, as it is more likely you will hit upon what works best for the child and family. Think about carrying a more substantial bag of creative resources with you. I have a couple of portable art boxes that travel with me in my car boot together with a large oil cloth to cover tables and floors and allay anxieties about making too much mess. I always have baby wipes handy too, for wiping messy hands, faces and accidental spillages at the end of the sessions.

The most used art box contains a range of good quality art materials – Crayola Twistables (then you never need a pencil sharpener), Sharpies, fine liners and a range of art pencils for basic contained drawing tasks. I also have chalk and oil pastels and charcoal sticks, but these are much more expressive materials so need to be used with more care. I tend not to offer paint on home visits or in school settings, but I do have a set of paint dabbers; it's much harder to make a horrible mess with these. I also avoid tubs of glitter for similar reasons, having once had a child empty a full pot onto the carpeted school library floor. It seems not everyone finds glitter remains sparkling in the carpet pretty. I do however have a craft box containing googly eyes, sequins and sparkles, a selection of stickers, tissue paper squares and circles, pipe cleaners, pompoms, glue sticks and left- and right-handed scissors of various sizes for children and adults. In the second box I have more tactile materials for making 3D objects such as self-hardening clay, Playdoh and Plasticine, together with a range of cutting and moulding tools. The clay provides a soothing experience for some, and can be accessed and modelled without sophisticated fine motor skills. Be mindful of the setting when using these materials and of making the area both safe to use and easy to clean up.

I also keep a bag full of diverse magazines; some child-friendly ones like *CBeebies* or *Match* and free ones from supermarkets and travel agents. These can be used for lots of activities (e.g. Life Graph in Chapter 5) and are great to use with children and adults who lack confidence in their own art making or creative capacity. I keep a range of paper in an art folder, as this seems the best way of maintaining it in good condition. Make sure you have some smaller A4 as well as larger (A3 or bigger) sheets of paper in a range of colours; some people can feel overwhelmed when faced with a large piece of paper, unsure how to fill it, whilst others will need more space to express themselves. Some young people like to work in a sketch pad, and this is good to leave with them if you feel they could benefit from a space to express themselves between sessions or if you are working together over a longer period.

I also have a large cloth bag with lots of smaller matching cloth bags inside, containing a range of small toys, thanks to my lovely friend and colleague Athaliah Durrant who made it for me when I joined our team. Having the smaller bags inside means it's easier for you to select items for children in advance, and they are less likely to be overwhelmed by choice. The little bags are themed: cars and emergency vehicles, dinosaurs, animal families, human figures, wrestlers, monsters, soft toys and puppets, etc. You can use them in so many ways during assessments: to observe independent free play or interactions between parent and child; for occupational play or to comfort younger children where there may be a lack of appropriate toys/stimulation in the home while you speak with the parent/caregiver; or to facilitate some of the activities later in this book that rely on the use of miniatures both with children and adults (see Sculpting in Chapter 5, Doll's House in Chapter 6). It might also be useful for specific activities to have larger items like toy telephones or dolls (see Building Strong Walls in Chapter 8).

Whilst my bag is now filled to bursting, it didn't start off this way and I haven't bought any of the contents new. Before I had children, I scoured the 10 pence boxes in charity shops and at car boot sales, and since having children I have re-appropriated toys when they have outgrown them. It can also be nice to have a couple of storybooks with you or simple games like Jenga to start or finish a direct work session.

Assessing children and families with additional communication needs

In assessments, we are likely to come across many people who speak little or no English and who might be said to be in a linguistic minority: new arrivals to the country (predominantly refugees and asylum seekers); long-standing residents who haven't learnt to speak English or have forgotten what they once learnt; deaf people; and people with learning disabilities. The needs of these four groups are different but there are likely to be overlaps in terms of the skills needed in assessment, which will be explored here.

Culturally competent assessments

You will struggle to find practice guidance that isn't loaded with references to taking full account of ethnicity, culture and religion in assessments, but much less available is advice about *how* to take account of these issues so they are appropriately addressed. I wonder if there is an assumption that this will happen by following the same set of basic principles that apply to assessment in general practice? 'If the practice and the principles are right for every child, then they will take into account the needs of those children who have recognisably different cultural heritages' (Kennedy 2017, p.1).

Lack of knowledge, experience and understanding of how to deliver a culturally sensitive service can lead to assessments that lack depth, that fail to draw all information together to offer a holistic perspective, or most worryingly lead to practitioners making unhelpful assumptions about the culture or religion of the family. Littlechild (2012) talks about *cultural relativism*; the idea that an individual's beliefs, values and cultural practices should be understood on the basis of that person's own culture rather than being judged against criteria imposed by another. An example of a worst-case scenario was the case of Victoria Climbié, where forms of cultural relativism resulted in her social worker ascribing the child's unusual behaviour of standing to attention when her aunt visited her in hospital as culturally explicable: indicative of respect and obedience for elders often seen in African-Caribbean families. Where practitioners have limited or subjective knowledge of a particular culture, potentially abusive or dangerous practices can be falsely attributed to aspects of cultural life (DoH 2009).

Laming (DoH 2009) was clear that we can never justify detrimental parenting practices or abusive behaviour towards children by making assumptions about culture or religion. Other Serious Case Reviews have reported that racial stereotyping has at times prevented practitioners from fully assessing fathers. In the case of Jasmine Beckford, her father's views about his parenting role, education, discipline and punishment were never sought before he went on to kill his daughter. Were workers scared of violence from this man or fearful of allegations of racist practice? (Dutt and Phillips 2010). As recently as 2015, Ofsted, in its review of effective assessment practices, highlighted that the 'diverse populations in some authorities created barriers to effective working due to a lack of understanding by the local authority staff of the cultures of some minority ethnic groups' (Ofsted 2015, p.20). Ofsted also noted that there was an occasional reluctance by certain groups to engage with statutory services.

Generalised assumptions about cultural patterns or commonalities, whilst a useful starting point, are no substitute for assessing the meaning of ethnicity, culture or faith in a family. This is a field where it is vital to learn from and work with communities to develop competent practice. For example, what does it mean to be a Muslim girl in this home? How does being a Bangladeshi boy in this school and community impact on educational chances? Let us avoid assumptions. Stereotypical or simplistic views of difference – ethnicity, class, disability, language or religion – have no place in collaborative assessments. Littlechild's research (2012) highlights the need to understand the theory of 'otherness' to avoid discriminating against different ethnic and cultural groups and to support practitioners to work positively with difference. This translates into having respect and understanding for the experiences of people from other cultural backgrounds in order to communicate and work effectively with them in assessment. It is important to hear the stories or narratives of children and their families in order to understand their situation, their background and the influences that their culture, ethnicity and faith will inevitably have on them and on the development of their cultural identity or sense of sameness and belonging.

Littlechild (2012) also highlighted a trend in relation to safeguarding towards regarding BME families as having 'weaknesses' rather than 'strengths'. However, when we fully interrogate the meaning of culture or faith for children and their families, we are more likely to uncover beliefs that positively influence parenting and family life. Many BME families come from communities where the relationship between individual, family and community differs from a traditional Western narrative, and this must be acknowledged and understood. In assessments, we may identify that membership of a community – faith, BME or refugee and those seeking asylum – offers parents and children a support network and a sense of belonging and identity. To conclude:

> Problems can occur through translations leading to limited under-standings or total misunderstanding. Different cultures have different

ways of communicating respect and politeness. Expressions, dress codes and non-verbal behaviour can be acceptable in one culture but can sometimes be insulting in another; for example, proximity and eye contact…when communicating professionals should always be aware of difference in culture ethnicity and social groups, be respectful and act without prejudice. (Dunhill 2009, p.22)

Working with interpreters

A note now about working in assessments through an interpreter where English is not the service user's first language. Consider the practical arrangements first of all.

- Does your service have access to trained interpreters?

- Are you familiar with booking arrangements and fees? Who is responsible for payment?

- Identify the language and dialect spoken by the service user.

- Check whether the interpreters and translators have been assessed for their competency in spoken interpretation and/or written translation.

- Double-check that the interpreter and service user speak the same language or dialect.

- Observe the gender and religious preferences of the service user when arranging for an interpreter.

Then, in the session, bear in mind the following key factors. It is not acceptable to use family members, members of the local community or friends to interpret for you, especially not children interpreting for their parents. This role must be impartial and independent. You need to allow time for a pre-interview discussion with the interpreter to talk about the content of the session and the way in which you wish to work. Ensure that you have discussed any complex or professional terms that you will use before the session so interpreters can familiarise themselves with them and check back with you for clarification and/ or misunderstanding. Encourage the interpreter to ask questions and to interrupt you if necessary for points of clarification, especially if the service user hasn't understood the question. Although you may feel this interrupts the flow or your train of thought, it is preferable to your words being misinterpreted or to the interpreter acting as a mediator or adding examples of his own for clarification. To minimise the likelihood of this happening, try to use straightforward language and avoid jargon.

Actively listen to the interpreter and the service user, trying to maintain eye contact with him and not with the interpreter. You will of course need more time for your session or to manage your expectations of how much information you will cover. At the end of the session, check whether the service user has understood everything. Encourage him to ask questions or to write them down in his own language to be discussed the next time you meet. Don't then rush off at the end. It is important to have a post-interview discussion with the interpreter, to check that the session went according to your needs and the needs of the service user, and to find out whether any changes need to be made for the next time you meet. Don't forget that these sessions can be very distressing for interpreters, as well as for children and families. The chance to debrief after the session might be much appreciated.

Working with families with complex health needs or disabilities

When I was canvassing opinions from local social work teams about what they would find helpful in a book about creative assessment, there were many requests to include thinking about assessments of children and families with additional needs, complex health issues or disabilities. Part of the difficulty in this field of work, is that there is no definition of what constitutes complexity of need in children. 'Government guidance describes a continuum of needs and services, with children who have complex needs located at the top end of this continuum, as a subset of children with additional needs' (Marchant 2010, pp.200–201).

Children with disabilities qualify as children in need under Section 17(10) of the Children Act 1989. The available evidence would suggest disabled children are at increased risk of abuse and that the presence of multiple disabilities appears to increase the risk of abuse and neglect; yet there is an under-reporting of disabled children in the safeguarding system. A large-scale US study of over 40,000 children found that disabled children were 3.4 times more likely to be abused or neglected than non-disabled children. Overall the study concluded that 31 per cent of disabled children had been abused compared with 9 per cent of the non-disabled child population (cited in Murray and Osborne 2009).

Disabled children are also over-represented in the population of children in care, making up 10 per cent of all children in care in the UK, and are more likely to be in a residential rather than family setting, which also increases vulnerability due to multiple caregivers (Murray and Osborne 2009). Indicators of abuse can all too easily be explained away as a function of impairment; behaviours that could be indicative of emotional distress connected with abuse such as self-harm, sleep or eating difficulties can also be factors associated with a health condition, impairment or disability. Another difficulty for practitioners in assessment is sometimes in focusing on the needs of the child rather than the caregiver, who may at times be overwhelmed by his caregiving responsibilities.

So how do we understand this increased risk and vulnerability to experiencing abuse? There are many factors reported in Murray and Osborne's guidance (2009) which I summarise here:

- Disabled children generally have fewer contacts outside the home, and this increased social isolation means they may struggle to find opportunities to tell others about abuse.

- There is often dependency on parents/caregivers or paid carers for personal care and assistance in daily life.

- The ability to actively resist or avoid abuse may be impaired (e.g. limited mobility or speech and language difficulties).

- Communication needs may make it harder to tell someone about the abuse so it may endure for longer.

- Access to trusted adults may be limited.

- They are vulnerable to bullying and harassment which can be so severe as to constitute assault or abuse.

- There may be limited access to personal safety programmes and personal, sex, health and relationship education, resulting in a lack of awareness of what constitutes abusive treatment or consent issues.

Disabled children have the same rights and needs as all non-disabled children. 'There is no need to begin from a different place...

disabled children…need social workers who are able to communicate directly with them, involve them in decisions about their lives and make sense of the barriers they face' (Marchant 2008, p.158). But what has become clear to me is that although there is no magic wand or a one-size-fits-all solution, communication would appear once more to be at the heart of the issue. Children are as different in their experiences of disability and complex needs as they are in all their experiences. In all cases, good assessment is critical in identifying and meeting these children's needs. As a bottom line, you must believe that all children with complex needs have the same rights and needs as children without, so you should approach your assessment adhering to the same guidelines and principles. These additional pointers will help you (adapted from Koprowska 2008):

- Get to know what suits the individual and adjust your pace and communication style accordingly.

- Avoid complex grammar, ambiguous terminology or idiom.

- Check out the person's understanding and ensure you don't reach a decision without his full involvement.

- Respect the person's chosen form of communication (e.g. British Sign Language as a full and complex language).

- Allow more time for meetings; be patient.

- Use interpreters, especially for critical assessment sessions and meetings.

- Offer creative means of communication: pen and paper, gesture, drawing.

- Form words clearly and don't cover your mouth when speaking.

- Where possible learn skills in pictorial or non-verbal communication (e.g. Makaton, PECS).

In assessment terms, there will undoubtedly be additional information required related to a disability and/or health needs. You must be clear about the nature of the difficulties; people reading your assessment don't just need a list of diagnoses taken from a medical dictionary. As well as defining the child's (or adult's) condition, you should describe how this impacts his life: How does it manifest and does it limit or affect him? How does it make him feel? What is the social and emotional impact? How do environmental adaptations or treatment plans impact his life? Does medication make a difference in terms of his capacity to engage – perhaps this is harder just before or after taking it? Marchant (2008) writes:

> As a first step we need to travel to the child's understanding of their condition: what have they been told, what do they know, what more if anything do they want or need to know? We should not deny the reality of the child's impairment or condition but neither should we assign it unnecessary significance. (p.165)

As with all children and families, be prepared to tailor your approach and your resources to the cognitive, communicative and motivational needs of the individual child or adult. In terms of verbal communication, it is important to be aware in assessments of the differences between *receptive* and *expressive* language.

Expressive language is the use of words in sentences to communicate with other people. Where people have difficulties in this area it could be related to word finding, putting words in the right order or being unable to form words so others can understand. From an assessment perspective, remember that someone with expressive language difficulties might find it hard to tell you a coherent story. He might become frustrated if he can't express himself in the way he wants or needs. He might not be able to repeat the story with the same level of detail or accuracy, which could be interpreted as being dishonest or untrustworthy when this isn't the case. This could be further compounded of course if the person has recently experienced a very traumatic event.

Receptive language is the understanding of expressive language or comprehension. The use of receptive language is not dependent on being able to use expressive language and vice versa. A person might not be able to form words or sentences, but can understand everything that is said to him. Conversely, I have known many children who can speak in full sentences with a wide-ranging vocabulary, but may at times struggle to understand or process what is being said to them.

Some people can use both expressive and receptive language to varying degrees whilst others may be able to use one or the other (Foundation for People with Learning Disabilities n.d.). It is also worth noting that it is very common for young children to experience speech and language difficulties – as many as one child in ten under five years old – but that many then catch up without further input. Others of course will have a more significant and persistent difficulty with longer-term impact (DfES 2005). Ultimately, as far as assessments are concerned, don't make assumptions about understanding; ask.

Body language is another vital part of communication and is thought to convey at least half of what we are saying. When adults talk they also tend to use gestures alongside words. For some people with communication difficulties, this can be crucial in helping them interpret and navigate the world, including understanding simple everyday interactions. For others, for example people with autistic spectrum disorders, reading body language might represent more of a challenge. They might also struggle with eye contact, reading non-verbal cues and recognising personal space boundaries.

When working with people who have a disability, there are some helpful premises in *I am Special* by Peter Vermeulen (2013), a workbook designed to help children and adults with autism spectrum disorders understand their diagnosis, gain confidence and thrive. He writes: 'A disability means that certain activities (not all) are more complex than for others, or even impossible. A person with a disability, then, feels disabled in certain situations, but not in others.' As part of your assessment, you will need to identify what solutions and aids the person has devised for themselves or has accessed to help with the problems and difficulties they experience. For example, does the person lipread? Does he use specific aids or have environmental adaptations that make life better or easier. Although information gathering may need to take longer, by making reasonable adjustments you will gain a much clearer understanding of what is going on.

In terms of communication techniques make it your business to establish what works for the individual; rather than asking 'Does he talk?' ask 'How do you communicate?' This could be by using an augmentative and alternative communication (ACC) system, such as Widgit, Makaton (based on British Sign language) or PECS (picture exchange communication system), which supplements or replaces speech and handwriting. It might be a voice output communication aid (VOCA); these include a large range of devices that speak, from simple single-message systems to more sophisticated technology that is advancing year on year. Don't overlook the obvious either: a text, letter or email.

Ensure you give enough time for the information you have shared or for what you have said to be processed, particularly for people with learning disabilities, before you move on. Do this by creating pauses, explaining one idea or concept or asking one question at a time. You might also need to talk more slowly, using simpler language and sentence structure, and certainly avoid jargon, idiom and euphemism. Concrete visual props or cues can be helpful in reinforcing understanding of what you're trying to convey. You need to ensure that materials are available in an accessible format, making it easier to read, with shorter sentences and visual prompts (Easy Read) or using photo symbols.

Then make sure you check and re-check the person has understood, perhaps by asking, 'Could you please tell me what I just said so I can be certain I've explained it to you well enough?' 'Can I please make sure you're clear about what's happening tomorrow?' 'Can you show me using these photos who will be coming to the meeting?' This is sometimes called creating feedback loops. At appropriate times rephrase and mirror what the person has said. You can then ask further questions or build on what has been discussed already. This is a great way of acknowledging or checking you have understood or providing clarification where necessary. By using a feedback loop, you can confirm the communication has been accurately received. I also find repetition is vital. Always recap the session at the end of your meeting and recap again when you next meet. You may similarly need to repeat activities in the same way or with slight variations.

If you're struggling to make yourself understood, think about the setting – do you need to be somewhere less noisy? Are there too many distractions? Does the person need support from an advocate or someone who knows him better to support understanding – a teacher, parent/carer or spouse? Where there are issues with engagement, look to yourself to see where the difficulty lies: what is it that you are not getting quite right that means you are not able to effectively communicate with someone? Rather than thinking 'this person is not engaging', reframe this to 'I haven't managed to engage him yet.' Take responsibility for addressing this problem, rather than locating the difficulty in the individual.

I will never forget as a newly qualified social worker preparing for a review of short breaks for a 17-year-old boy with cerebral palsy, whom I will call John. He was blind, in a wheelchair and had little speech. Whenever I visited I would say 'Hello', John would vocalise to let me know he had heard me, and I would then speak with his mother. When it came to gaining John's views about the short breaks, I felt completely out of my depth in knowing how to communicate with him and seek his views. His mother had a learning disability and mental health difficulties and didn't feel able to help me, and his father had died many years before. So, I went to school and met with John with his class teacher. With her support, John answered all my questions; she was so skilled at asking in a way that gave him simple options for replying. Knowing him as well as she did, she could also interpret his vocalisations in a way I could not. He had been having short breaks since he was a very little boy and I learned at the review that this was the first time his views had been represented, and that he was present as his views were shared by the person he chose to share them.

There will be times when you will need the support of a third party. With the best will in the world it would be impossible to be trained in all available means to assist communication. If a child signs, for example, and you don't, you will need an interpreter. In other situations, you might just need to know there is someone around who could help if you hit a stumbling block to communication. Where possible, it is better to involve the child in the choice of who supports the meeting and, if you will be meeting on several occasions, better that this person is consistent.

Where parents or carers have a learning disability

Of course, when we are talking about child and family assessments, we must include all the above factors for parents and caregivers too. Your agency may have its own guidelines for working with parents with a learning disability; but if not, I direct you here to some helpful resources. It is first important to quantify what we mean when we talk about a *learning disability*, a term traditionally used within the social care statutory framework. It is defined by MENCAP as 'a reduced intellectual ability and difficulty with everyday activities – for example household tasks, socialising or managing money – which affects someone for their whole life'. In contrast, *learning difficulties* is a term more typically utilised in special educational needs frameworks, and the two definitions are not interchangeable. A learning difficulty, like dyslexia, does not affect intellect.

People with a learning disability may take longer to learn or need additional support to develop new skills or behaviours. They may find it harder to understand complex concepts or information and to interact with others. The level of support needed will vary from person to person as learning disabilities can be mild, moderate or severe/profound. A particular level of IQ is not the sole characteristic of a learning disability, as individuals can demonstrate different abilities across different components of the IQ and other diagnostic tests.

> There is no clear relationship between IQ and parenting, unless it is less than 60 (McGaw and Newman 2005). However, although IQ is not a good indicator of parenting capacity, cognitive impairment may mean that a parent has difficulty with reading and writing, remembering and understanding, decision making and problem-solving, and this will create particular support needs. (WTPN 2016)

Where a learning disability is suspected you should use an initial screening tool to determine whether further specialist assessment is needed. It can be especially difficult to diagnose a mild learning disability as the individual may cope well in certain aspects of life and just need support with small pockets of functioning. Be mindful of the potential stigma attached to having a learning disability when addressing this with parents/carers. It may be useful to frame the issue in terms of identification of possible support needs. In relation to this, consider whether the parent would benefit from an independent advocate during the assessment sessions.

Where a parent/caregiver has a learning disability, consider a PAMS (Parent Assessment Manual Software: McGaw 2016) assessment. PAMS is a methodical, functional guide used by social workers to work with families where there are safeguarding concerns, offering techniques for assessors to use when working with adults with learning disabilities or difficulties. It will include exploration of a parent's knowledge of parenting, observations of parent and child together, and feedback from the parent, as well as from other agencies.

I would also recommend you look at:

- *Learning Curves*, a manual for practitioners to support the assessment of parents with learning difficulties (Morgan and Goff 2004)

- Working Together with Parents Network (www.wtpn.co.uk), which supports professionals working with parents who have learning difficulties or disabilities

- British Institute of Learning Disabilities (www.bild.org.uk), which offers a full range of resources to ensure people with learning disabilities are equally valued and participate fully in their communities

- *The Court and Your Child: When Social Workers Get Involved* – accessible information for parents available free of charge from CHANGE (www.changepeople.org.uk).

In 2016, the Working Together with Parents Network updated the DoH/DfES *Good Practice Guidance on Working with Parents with a Learning Disability* (2007), which was by then out of date. This can be found at www.basw.co.uk. The original guidance set out five principles of good practice which are:

- provision of accessible information and communication

- clear and coordinated referral, assessment and eligibility criteria

- support designed to meet assessed need of parents and their children

- long-term support if this is needed

- access to an independent advocacy service.

The guidance is clear that information about universal services should be available to parents with learning disabilities in formats that suit their needs. For example, Easy Read versions of leaflets, audio or visual information, fully accessible websites and face-to-face opportunities to learn about services for parents or prospective parents, across the different stages of their child's life. Making information accessible can help with reducing fear about asking for help. Hold in your mind, especially when reviewing previous referrals or assessments, that if additional needs have not previously been identified that this may have impacted on families making progress with plans or engaging with support.

Key messages for social workers who want to be successful in communicating with parents with a learning disability are:

- Be respectful.

- Be on time.

- Speak directly to parents.

- Don't use jargon – speak in plain English.

- Think before you talk.

- Listen and really 'hear' what is being said.

- Explain clearly what is happening.

- Be honest if you can't help.

- Be patient.

- Make enough time to communicate effectively.

(adapted from WTPN 2016, p.7)

CHAPTER 3

EXPLORING PROTECTIVE FACTORS IN CHILDREN AND FAMILIES

Strengths and Resilience

When working with vulnerable children and their families, we are always considering the scales of balance between positive and negative factors in their lives. When we make judgements or decisions about risk, we must do so in the context of an evidence-based framework that allows us to look at resilience and protective factors against those risks. We are also increasingly aware of the impact of adverse childhood experiences (ACEs), since the first UK study in 2012. This study (Bellis *et al.* 2014a) found that exposure to a higher number of ACEs before your 18th birthday was strongly associated with unfavourable behavioural, health and social outcomes. A subsequent national study the following year found at least half the general population has one ACE and 8 per cent had four or more, which would be considered as significantly heightened vulnerability (Bellis *et al.* 2014b). There are three types of ACEs, highlighting ten types of childhood trauma:

- *Abuse*: physical, emotional, sexual

- *Neglect*: physical, emotional

- *Household dysfunction*: mental illness, mother treated violently, relative in prison, parental separation or divorce, household substance abuse.

ACEs significantly increase health risks on many levels:

- *Behaviour:* lack of physical activity, smoking, alcoholism, drug use and missed work

- *Physical and mental health:* severe obesity, diabetes, depression, suicide attempts, sexually transmitted disease, heart disease, cancer, stroke, COPD and broken bones.

(Felitti *et al.* 1998)

The ACE Pyramid (Figure 3.1) represents the conceptual framework for the original ACE study (Felitti *et al.* 1998).

Figure 3.1 The ACE Pyramid
(adapted from Felitti et al. *1998)*

An ACE score is a tally of different types of abuse, neglect and adversity, but it isn't a crystal ball, simply guidance. Considering ACEs alone also doesn't account for the positive experiences in early life that can build resilience and provide a buffer against the impact of trauma. This could be having an aunt that loves you and provides nurture, or having a mentor in school or within the community you can confide in. Having resilience is a protective factor and can benefit children and adults who have been exposed to trauma or who have high ACE scores – over 4 out of 10 (you can access the ACE score calculator at www.acestudy.org).

The impact of any negative experience on a child also depends on the nature of the experience. To more fully explore ACEs for any individual you should consider some clarifying questions/information (Gilligan 2010):

- The age and stage of the child, contextual factors and the child's temperament before the event.

- How were things going before the event and did the child have access to support?

- What was the immediate context to the critical experience?

- In the aftermath did the child have access to key supportive adults? How did he respond immediately and over time? Did the support remain available across home, school, friendship group, community?

- What was the balance of adversity and protection at different times – preceding, during and after the event?

It is important in assessments to be looking across all aspects of a child and family's life to consider resilience as well as adversity, be it in school or employment, through friendships, building social skills and leisure opportunities or through participation and responsibility.

> Whether it is considered an outcome, a process or a capacity, the essence of resilience is a positive, adaptive response in the face of adversity. It is neither an immutable trait nor a resource that can be used up. On a biological level, resilience results in healthy development because it protects the developing brain and other organs from the disruptions produced by excessive activation of stress response systems. Stated simply, resilience transforms potentially *toxic* stress into *tolerable* stress. In the final analysis, resilience is rooted in both the physiology of adaptation and the experiences we provide for children that either promote or limit its development. (National Scientific Council on the Developing Child 2015, p.1)

Resilience is a key factor in promoting wellbeing and good mental health; the quality of being able to deal with life's ups and downs. It is more likely to occur when services, support and health resources are made available to allow children and families to do well in ways that are psychologically, culturally, socially and physically meaningful to them.

Gilligan (1997) identifies three fundamental building blocks of resilience:

- a secure base – where the child feels a sense of belonging and security

- good self-esteem – an internal sense of worth and competence

- self-efficacy – a sense of mastery and control as well as a realistic understanding of your strengths and limitations.

Within these building blocks are six domains:

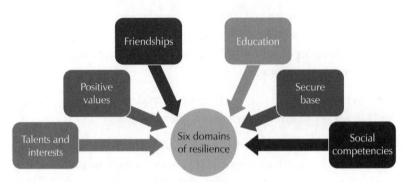

Figure 3.2 The six domains of resilience
(adapted from Gilligan 1997)

When considering resilience, it's helpful to think about and understand the impact of each domain on functioning, against the assessment framework (DoH 2000). By relating this resilience model back to the framework, you can be sure you are integrating a strengths-based approach and giving sufficient weight to understanding the significance of resilience factors. Don't forget that these may be external protective factors (e.g. a supportive teacher or neighbour) as well as internal resilience (e.g. determination). Your plan can then influence strengthening the child's and family's resources, perhaps through a Family Group Conference, as well as reducing harm.

Understanding resilience factors in children and their families is a crucial element when later planning your intervention. Your plans need to include consideration of external protective factors as well as internal resources in the context of adversity as well as protective factors in the child's ecology: family, friends, community and environment. Don't ignore the cultural frame either to avoid your focus being limited to Western notions of risk and resilience. You will need to identify factors to maximise (to build resilience and safety) as well as those factors to minimise (to reduce risk and vulnerability).

Ultimately it is the everyday experiences children and young people have with caregivers and educators that provide the best opportunities for reinforcing self-esteem and building resilience; so when you are liaising with the child's systemic network, notice whether this is happening as often as it should through praise, encouragement and *affection*. These are the things that over time will help to create a core belief in a child and a felt sense that he is loveable and worthwhile. Children who feel this are typically more confident and secure. They are better able to manage stressors in their lives and to manage new situations or challenges with confidence, composure and hope.

Where children have impaired self-esteem and resilience, *achievement* – or 'the ability to transform ideas into actions' (Grotsky *et al.* 2000, p.71) – is also compromised. These children feel defeated before they have even begun. Children who have been shamed or humiliated become easily frustrated when things don't immediately go according to plan. Sometimes they worry they will be punished for failure. How much is this a factor in the child and family you're assessing?

Working with children and families, we can explore resilience as something that has contributed to them having influence over their lives, over a problem or difficulty. If we search for resilient qualities in people, this can lead to a shift in perception of the self. We might ask questions about the inner qualities that he taps into at times of stress or difficulty (e.g. perseverance, bravery, logical thinking) and enquire how, despite the challenges, the person has kept going. We can also ask questions about what actions he has been able to take because of these qualities. For example, 'What has being brave allowed you to do, that you might otherwise not have done?' Or ask about a time when he dealt successfully with a problem that could have stopped him moving forward.

To assess strengths and resilient factors in a child or family, it is always better to see them rather than hear about them. Engaging in activities together will really enhance this as you will see how individuals manage challenges, cope with disappointments, use their creativity, persevere if things don't go according to plan and share enjoyment. In this chapter you will find activities that will help you explore strengths, resilient qualities and self-esteem within individuals and family groups and communities.

COMBINED SKILLS AND STRENGTHS

 Materials

Paper, pens, glue or stapler.

Process

This is a good parent/caregiver activity that will help you look at the skills and strengths of individuals within the family unit as well as within the family itself. It is also an opportunity to assess whether hostile or conflicting interpersonal interactions may impact on successful problem-solving. You will be asking the family to focus on its assets, rather than on its problems. You will be interested in establishing whether caregivers can work together to become more conscious of skills, knowledge and values held within the family system.

Take an A4 sheet of paper and cut it in half in a zigzag vertically.

Figure 3.3 Combined skills and strengths zigzag

Give one half to each caregiver with a heading across the top of *combined strengths and skills*. Each partner should then compose a list of his or her strengths and skills as close to the cut as possible. You might need to prompt them in respect of the skills or strengths they might like to include, for example personal qualities or skills they could share or pass on to their children. If you have some knowledge of the individuals you could highlight things you have noticed, for example that the dad is very playful with his toddler or that he is supportive of his partner accessing education. When each caregiver has completed his or her half independently, join the paper together again using staples or glue. Use this document to then begin a discussion about how they can work together to address any issues or problems in the family system.

An alternative with carers who might be struggling to identify strengths and skills would be to have some laminated cards with different strengths on each. Put them in a box and ask each parent/caregiver to take turns in pulling cards out randomly. Can they then decide which parent is best at each thing and discard any that are unsuitable? You could also use this activity with children and young people. Make sure you have a combination of functional strengths, particularly in relation to parenting such as helping with homework or making the dinner as well as non-functional tasks like being playful or giving hugs.

✓ Aims

- To promote a positive outlook and perception of the family as a unit.

- To assess family cohesion – can the family work as a team? Can the 'problems' be set aside temporarily to focus on a task together?

- To empower parents/caregivers and assess skills in working independently as problem-solvers.

- To increase understanding of why difficulties may have arisen in the family system.

Handy hints

The exercise outlined above assumes a two-parent family and you will need to consider how you might adapt it for separated parents or single parents. Could the separated parents come together to work on the exercise? Does a single parent draw in help from a friend, neighbour or relative to support with the parenting task?

When we work with families to facilitate doing an activity together, working towards a non-problem-focused goal, some family problems can improve simply by focusing on more positive stories. These sorts of activities can promote cooperation and communication between family members or sibling groups. As well building up family cohesion they can also illuminate negative communication patterns, problems with regulation of feelings and poor problem-solving capacity. This information is crucial for planning interventions together.

This exercise is adapted from Ollier and Hobday (1999).

IDENTIFYING PERSONAL NETWORKS

✂ Materials

Paper, pens (sequins, stickers or other collage materials are optional for decoration). You might want to bring a prepared template of a hand, ladder, flower or umbrella.

✎ Process

In life we all need a personal network; a group of people who is there to celebrate with us when times are good and to support us when we need them, for whatever reason. This exercise will help you explore with a child or adult whether he has an adequate, containing support system.

There are various options for this exercise depending on the age, gender and interests of the child, the most commonly used being the Hand of Safety. I like to use the child's own hand to draw around or I might have a generic hand template ready. Other ideas are to use a flower with five or six petals or an umbrella or ladder with a similar number of different sections.

Figure 3.4 Personal Networks examples

Tell the child that you would like to learn about the safe people in his life; who he would go to if he was worried, scared or had a problem. Ask the child to try to identify five safe people and write their names on the individual fingers of the hand. You will be reinforcing the importance of these people throughout the session, so encourage the child to decorate the hand to reflect its importance.

Martin (2007) suggests the criteria for being a network person is an adult who will listen, believe, be available and accessible and take action if required to protect the child and help him feel safe once more. Although it is not necessary to be this prescriptive, she develops the idea further and suggests:

> using the thumb for an adult that lives in your home, second and third fingers for school staff and the fourth and fifth fingers for family or community members not living in the same home, for example another parent (if not living in the home), grandparent, neighbour, aunts or uncles or adults at out of school activities, (e.g. sport coach, scout leader) parents of friends, church leaders, family doctor etc. (Martin, 2007, p.13)

If you are doing the exercise with a child or young person and you suspect he has suffered or is suffering harm, use the process to also reinforce the idea from the protective behaviours model that children should persist in seeking help until they feel certain that someone has listened, understood and helped them to feel safe again (see also Wrench 2016). It is important during this exercise to stress that if the first person he asks doesn't help (he may not believe him or be busy dealing with another problem), he must try someone else in his network. The child will only know his problem has been dealt with when he feels safe again. You might need to role-play different scenarios with the child practising asking for help and persevering if he feels not heard. It's also important to emphasise that it's okay to break the rules in an emergency to get an adult's attention straight away, for example by interrupting a conversation, by saying 'no' or by breaking a secret. This might ultimately support a child or young person to talk about what is happening that means he feels unsafe. You can then talk about what it is about each person that helps the child to feel safe or whether he would go to different people for different problems. Think about whom the child will be able to talk to about difficult feelings the work with you might engender during the assessment process too.

✓ Aims

– To create a systemic view of safety and support that can help increase the child's feelings of security.

– To learn more about the child's view of his support network and what 'safety' means to him.

help the child identify safe people if he is struggling to do
is and to explore what being a safe person means. How could
hese people support the child to keep safe?

— To explore the concept of persistence in the pursuit of safety
and reinforce the idea that it is okay to talk to an adult if you
are unsafe.

— If using this with a parent/caregiver much of the above applies,
but you could also look to understand existing support systems
and access to help during difficult times.

✋ Handy hints

Children will sometimes only want to include friends, pets or
siblings on their Hand of Safety; these are not network people.
It will be important for you to check out who the person is
before the name goes on the image, particularly given that some
children will want to name known perpetrators of abuse, and
adolescents will usually want to include their peers. Try to ensure
that the child has identified a range of adults in different settings
– home, school, short breaks placement, after school club, etc.

Within the session we sometimes write letters together to
the people in the child's network to encourage them to support
the child with keeping safe and to let them know the child has
identified them to be in his network. This should mean these
individuals will be more likely to respond quickly to the child's
overtures for help or support which, of course, are not always
explicitly made. Encourage the child to share good news with his
network people to open the lines of communication for when
they are most needed. You could also rehearse different scenarios
where he might need to contact his network person.

If you are involved with the child over a longer period, from
time to time have a Network Review as people can come and
go from children's lives and it's important to make sure the child
then updates his network as appropriate. He may have a change
of social worker or move classes in school at the end of the year,
for example. Others on the network may have been tried and
found wanting. On a positive note, new people may come into
children's lives who would be perfect network members.

There is no reason why you might not do a similar activity with adult family members to look at their systemic networks of support.

STRENGTHS-BASED ALL ABOUT ME

✂ Materials

A large sheet of drawing paper or ideally good-quality lining paper that the child can lie on, marker pens (other collage materials such as glitter, glue, stickers, coloured paper – optional).

✐ Process

This exercise can be done with individual children, sibling groups or parent/carer–child dyads. Ask the child to lie on the piece of paper and use a marker pen to draw around him, so that his body outline is on the paper. If the parent is the room, consider asking him to draw around the child. From here you can use the drawing in many different ways. The child can make a self-portrait, deciding what clothes to wear, how to style his hair, etc. He can record important facts about himself around the drawing such as his birthday or place of birth, as well as what he likes and is successful at. You could measure his height or weight and add that to the picture or ask him how he would describe himself. If the carers, parents or other siblings are present, ask them to add positive comments or funny stories and anecdotes about the child. The outcome should be a colourful and informative image to represent the child as he is now and a celebration of his strengths, resilience and achievements.

✓ Aims

– To build a relationship with the child and learn something about who he is now, his likes and dislikes. This can contribute to your understanding of a day in the life of this child in this family.

– To show your interest in the child and his world; crucial to building trust in the assessment relationship.

– To explore the child's strengths and resilient qualities – can he identify any for himself? Can the parent/carer notice these qualities in the child? How does the child receive praise or compliments? How does he receive criticisms if they, too, emerge?

- To observe interactions between parent/carer and child/ren and between siblings. If there is more than one child present, how does the parent share his time/resources? Does one child dominate? Does a particular child elicit more positive parental responses? Does the child seek parental approval? Does this child ask for adult help?

- To assess parenting capacity – can the parent ensure safety in the task? Do you observe emotional warmth? Does the parent give the child a sense of being valued? Does the parent communicate with the child? Does the parent help the child to regulate during the activity – including offering guidance and boundaries but also allowing the child to be creative within the task?

👍 Handy hints

It may not be appropriate to draw around the child if you suspect (or know) he has been sexually abused or is uncomfortable with such close physical proximity to you. You may be better advised to draw a generic outline of a body or ask the child to draw one and use this in the same way.

This activity can also help to explore identity with the child as he can see a physical representation of himself; how tall he is, how much space he takes up, as well as working out the sorts of things that make him who he is. This is key to understanding the child's sense of self within an assessment.

Finding out what children like and dislike or their favourite things (colour, pet, TV programme, ice cream flavour, etc.) and what makes them special can be done with simple worksheets as well. I often share some of my favourite things with the child too; for some children this is an important part of building up trust.

THE MEMORY BANK

✂ Materials

Something to hold the memories – a shoebox, glass jar or cardboard box, A4 paper and pens. You might want to bring craft materials if you decide to extend the task to include decoration of the memory bank. You could use little luggage labels or post-it notes to capture the memories.

If you opt for the extension exercise, leaf-shaped cardboard cut-outs are optional.

✎ Process

If time permits, first make or decorate the memory bank, so it can be claimed by the child/family as special. This is a good opportunity with a family group to observe how individuals manage a collaborative task. Offer a range of options for decoration if you can, including stickers or craft materials. Notice whether they can share enjoyment of the task. Who is taking charge? Can the adult maintain boundaries and ensure everyone is listened to and can contribute?

The decoration phase is a time to begin to generate discussion about family stories. You can lead this initially by prompting with some of your memories of the family or observations. You might prompt them to talk about a family photo in the room or a holiday period just gone. You might ask for best and worst memories for everyone in the family group. Notice the family's resourcefulness; has it become closed down so they are unable to respond in effective ways to problem-solve or can you gain access to the family's contexts of competence to create more expanded and useful accounts of the difficulties (Wilson 1998)?

After the decoration, it's time to capture some of those memories to put in the bank – make sure you offer options for how to do this. It could be drawing a picture, writing a few words on a luggage label or asking you to write the story down. Where memories of the same event are different, this must be normalised if we are to avoid a potential family argument. Tait and Wosu (2016) suggest making a memory string like bunting that captures different perspectives, with everyone's version of events represented.

Figure 3.5 Memory string

I think this would be a great intervention in and of itself if you are trying to establish the story around a particular incident that may need further investigation. It could also be a useful way of drawing together the various accounts of a 'problem' and help you understand how such 'problems' are defined, shaped and influenced through family interactions.

You could leave the box with the family and encourage them to add memories in the intervening period before your next visit. You can then take turns in pulling out the memories, making sure all have equal value. In recognising even small positives in people's lives, you help enable more positive representations of the self. However, you also open the door for people to share difficult feelings and memories that can be hard to access in the moment. This allows for voices to be heard that may otherwise be silenced.

✓ Aims

- To support the child or family to reflect on their experiences together and identify resilient qualities in individuals or as a family unit.

- To support reflection on vulnerabilities by remembering the past.

- If appropriate, to move on to thinking about how they might build on protective factors and minimise risks.

- To explore the child's strengths and resilient qualities – can he identify any for himself? Can the parent/carer notice these qualities in the child? How does the child receive praise or compliments? How does he receive criticisms if they too emerge?

- To observe interactions between parent/carer and child/ren and between siblings. If there is more than one child present, how does the parent share his time/resources? Does one child dominate? Does a particular child elicit more positive parental responses? Does the child seek parental approval? Does this child ask for adult help?

— To assess parenting capacity – can the parent ensure safety in the task? Do you observe emotional warmth? Does the parent give the child a sense of being valued? Does the parent communicate with the child? Does the parent help the child to regulate during the activity – including offering guidance and boundaries but also allowing the child to be creative within the task?

👍 Handy hints

Tait and Wosu (2016) also suggest you could adapt this into a Memory Tree if you haven't got a box to hand. You could use small tree branches in a jar or flower pot and then hang luggage labels on to the branches with the memories. Or you could draw a tree and use leaf-shaped pieces of paper to add the memories if you're really short on preparation time.

I think this is also a lovely activity to do with children in care when seeking their views before reviews. It will give you a snapshot of their lives but also of key relationships with caregivers.

THE TREE OF LIFE

✂ Materials

Pens and paper. A tree template with roots and branches is optional.

✏ Process

This is a tool typically used in narrative therapy developed originally for work with children orphaned by HIV/AIDS, but it has since been developed to work with people across the age range (Ncube 2007). Here I share versions of the exercise that will support you to learn more about strengths and resilience as well as risks and needs. Explain that the tree will be a metaphor for the person's life. Then draw an outline of a tree; make sure you have six component parts.

Roots

The ground

Trunk

Branches

Leaves

Fruits

You could use a pre-prepared template if you prefer. Talk about what the tree needs to survive; the roots take water from the soil to keep the tree alive and grow deep underground to anchor the tree and stop it from falling over in strong winds. A strong tree needs thick, sturdy, healthy roots that will carry on growing throughout the life of the tree, which adds to its safety and strength. The roots can symbolically represent where the person has come from, his family system, family name, stories about his past and ancestry. Then use this analogy to think about what the individual needs to help him feel secure and cared for. He can write the names of those people who look after him and keep him physically and emotionally safe on the roots, such as parents, friends or neighbours. Encourage him to think about what qualities he has of his own that keep him 'rooted' and strong, like persistence or determination.

The ground represents the here and now; everyday life, including activities, hobbies, interests, likes and dislikes, so encourage the person to add these to the image. Next move up to the trunk, which is the strongest part of the tree; ask him to write his strengths, resilient qualities and skills here. They are the parts of him that the world sees and others have most contact with, just like the tree trunk. For example, this could read, 'I did well in my SATs' or 'I stopped using heroin.'

Finally come up to the leaves and branches of the tree. Talk about how these are perhaps the prettiest parts of the tree, especially when swaying in the breeze or laden with blossom in the spring. When the seasons change, the leaves may die off, but they will always grow again the following year. In narrative therapy terms, the branches represent the individual's hopes, dreams and goals, while the leaves represent important people in his life. Again, you can prompt him to add these details to the image.

Sometimes the wind blows strongly and the branches get shaken. Ask what factors sometimes shake his 'leaves and branches'; what might stop him from staying strong and healthy? You can write these things or people on the leaves of the tree. For example, it could be a relationship, an agency (e.g. benefits) or financial worries. Finally, the fruits represent all the gifts the person has been given by others; they can be physical, psychological or social gifts.

✓ Aims

– To create a dialogue around family life, identity and the individual's lived experience.

– To identify risk and resilience factors and to problem-solve around this.

– To increase a sense of self-efficacy.

– To initiate conversations around resilience and stress as an assessment tool.

Handy hints

Remember that in simple terms, the roots represent resilient qualities and factors that minimise risk. The trunk symbolises the strengths and positive aspects of his life. The leaves and branches represent any risk factors or vulnerabilities.

In your planning you will need to think with the child/parent/carer about how to maximise strengths and resilience and how to minimise risk factors or stressors in their lives.

For more information and examples of the Tree of Life have a look at http://dulwichcentre.com.au/the-tree-of-life.

COUNT YOUR BLESSINGS

✂ Materials

Paper and drawing materials.

✐ Process

This is a simple activity suggested by Buchalter (2009) with a focus on the pleasures and positive aspects of life rather than problems, worries or frustrations. So, you should ask the child/adult to make an image that allows him to share his 'blessings' with you, in whichever form feels comfortable. If drawing is going to be an issue, you might bring a selection of magazines or clip-art images to choose from or to act as a prompt for those who struggle to identify positives in their lives.

✓ Aims

- To identify whether the person can identify positives; blessings can often be seen as achievements in life, such as having children, being successful in a team sport, maintaining good health, living in a lovely home.

- To explore whether the person can see his 'blessings' as significant in facing any challenges he has to deal with.

- Where possible, to begin to work on identifying ways in which to build on those 'blessings'.

☝ Handy hints

This exercise can be used with any age group, although with younger children you might need a different word to 'blessings' or at least to explain what 'blessings' means. It was originally used in a group therapy setting and could easily translate to a family or sibling group session. If so, you can either make a group, shared image on larger paper/lining paper, or each person can make his own image independently, which is shared at the end of the making period to reflect on whether there are shared experiences or themes within the work.

CHAPTER 4

EXPLORING AND UNDERSTANDING THE NATURE OF RELATIONSHIPS

In my experience as a social worker, practitioners are increasingly being asked to comment on, analyse and now offer an 'expert opinion' in court on *attachments* in families, and yet often our training has ill equipped us to observe and make sense of the interactions between parents/caregivers and their children. There is now much more awareness of theories around attachment and the impact of trauma and loss than when I did my social work diploma 20 years ago, but at times gaps still persist in knowledge around how to apply that theory to practice and to assessments in particular.

Most frequently we need to understand the nature of a relationship between a child and parent/caregiver or child and his siblings; I worry we can feel under pressure to make pronouncements about *attachment styles* and *attachment relationships* and yet lack a firm theoretical or research basis from which to reach our conclusions. As attachment processes are live across the lifespan, in assessing the needs of children and young people, this needs to begin with consideration of pregnancy, birth and infancy right through to adolescence and into adulthood. It is inevitable that it is often most challenging for us to try to understand the lived experience of infants and toddlers, probably because they are pre-verbal, but nonetheless, the *Framework for the Assessment of Children in Need and their Families* specifically highlights the need to consider 'the nature and quality of early attachments' when we are looking to assess a child's emotional and behavioural development (DoH 2000, p.19).

Different approaches and tools for the assessment of attachment are appropriate at different ages and stages of child development. Although Shemmings (2016a) highlights a growing range of evidence-based tools[1] they are not all readily available without further training and cost implications, leading to practitioners on occasion making assumptions about family relationships which are not evidence informed. With a lack of training in the assessment tools or lack of availability of such tools, we can only observe interactions between parents/caregivers and children, and sometimes our hypotheses are heavily influenced by our own attachment or relationship history or by our own cultural norms.

Assessing attachment is complex and requires formal training in the appropriate techniques. So, approach therefore with caution; if you're not formally trained, then it is most useful for you to make yourself familiar with attachment based behaviours and responses and use this to inform your assessment. To *assess* relationships and caregiving you need to *see* relationships and caregiving; looking at the inside and outside of these relationships.

Shemmings (2016b) gives some handy hints for practitioners in assessments about children and families. He advises us to consider whether we can use *relationship* instead of *attachment* in our thinking and in our assessments, as 'attachment' is such a precise term. For example: 'I have observed positives in the relationship between father and child such as...' It is important also to avoid using jargon like 'strong attachment' or 'attachment difficulties' and never to diagnose an 'attachment disorder' unless you have the relevant clinical experience and qualifications to do so.

---

1   The Parent Development Interview to assess a parent's internal working model of relationships (Aber *et al.* 1985); the Parent–Infant Relational Assessment Tool (PIRAT) suitable for systemising observations and pinpointing risk and areas of concern for infants and toddlers (Broughton 2010); as well as the Strange Situation procedure (Ainsworth and Wittig 1969). All these assessment tools require formal training in order to code them reliably. There are also various measures for older children, which include: Story Stem Completion (Hodges *et al.* 2003); the Child Attachment Interview (Target *et al.* 2003); and Attachment Q Sort (AQS). Additionally, there are measures for assessing caregiver behaviours: the Adult Attachment Interview (AAI: George *et al.* 1985); the Working Model of the Child Interview (Zeneah *et al.* 1996); Dissociative Experiences Scale; and the Disconnected and Extremely Insensitive Parenting (DIP) Measure (Out *et al.* 2009) (all cited in Shemmings 2016a).

Understanding attachment

Childcare professionals have long been using theories around attachment to inform their practice and understanding of human relationships. Although there are some cultural variations 'all humans share a common set of attachment needs – to have people close (primary carers) who act as a secure base and safe haven, with whom they want to spend time and separation from whom causes upset' (Shemmings 2016a, p.4). Depending on how these needs have or have not been met, attachment patterns emerge that form blueprints for further relationships throughout the lifespan. These patterns are evident from as early as four months of age but are not considered reliable or stable indicators before a child is a year old (Beebe *et al.* 2010).

It is important when gathering information about a child's developmental history that you include thinking about his pre-birth experiences. If you have a parent who can provide a safe base and who can hold his child in mind, that child learns empathy, theory of mind, social skills and to self-regulate. This child gains a template for healthy reciprocal relationships and is more likely to choose a partner who can offer empathy and stability before they choose to become parents (Silver 2013). Conversely, a parent with limited emotional resources is not always well equipped to set their own child up with the necessary resources. Whilst attachment patterns can and do often transmit through the generations, be aware that pregnancy can also be a catalyst for change. Parents can be highly motivated *not* to repeat intergenerational cycles of abuse and keen to have support to establish new parenting patterns. Typically, the caregiving system is activated during pregnancy and is experienced in parents to be as a strong urge to protect and nurture the unborn child or, in fathers, also to protect the mother-to-be.

Don't underestimate the importance of the impact of fathers on their infants and children. As well as sometimes being marginalised or problematised in social work, men can of course act as protective and resilient factors in children's lives. Remember that children can develop different attachment relationships with different caregivers. It is perfectly possible for children to have several attachment figures, but they tend to be organised hierarchically. The child might have a preferred caregiver to go to when upset (typically the mother), but if the mother wasn't available, he would go to the father, then the aunt, then the grandparent, etc., who might all offer different but still effective caregiving. 'Rather than the individual role of the father, it is the nature of the parental couple that creates the "emotional climate" into which an infant is born, that is likely to be more critical for the future mental health of the developing infant' (Shemmings 2016a, p.17).

When we are assessing vulnerable children and families, it is vital to be mindful of attachment-based behaviours, especially where there are safeguarding concerns, but such assessments are complex. Attachment has survival value; the child's physical and psychological safety relies on keeping the parent closest when the child is at his most vulnerable. When a child has a need (e.g. hunger or for comfort) or feels he is in danger or under threat, he has an automatic physiological and psychological response – he becomes emotionally aroused and dysregulated, which activates the attachment system. This in turn triggers attachment behaviours, designed to draw the parent/caregiver's attention to the need or to the child's distress. There are critical situations that elicit attachment behaviours including:

- illness or injury

- being alone or in darkness

- hunger

- tiredness

- presence of a stranger

- absence of primary caregiver (especially before six to seven months when the concept of object permanence is achieved – even if the parent isn't in sight, the infant knows the parent continues to exist and so avoids high anxiety).

Infant or child attachment behaviours include:

- crying

- clinging or holding

- following the caregiver with his eyes or making eye contact

- smiling

- protesting at separation

- reaching or seeking to be picked up

- signalling or calling to the caregiver.

These cycles are repeated innumerable times every day, and it is these repeated interactions that establish attachment bonds in the first three to five years if the primary carer is both accessible (physically and psychologically present and available) and responsive (with accuracy and sensitivity to the child's needs). By six to seven months of age, the infant's primary caregiver ought to have become the child's primary attachment figure, their 'go to' at times of need or distress (Howe 2010).

You should be familiar with one secure and two insecure (avoidant and ambivalent) patterns of behaviour that were originally identified using the results of the Strange Situation procedure (Ainsworth and Wittig 1969[2]). They are organised patterns of relating, each representing a set of consistent psychological and behavioural strategies the child employs to keep his parent/caregiver close by, to maximise care, survival and protection. Shemmings (2016a) reports an approximate 60:40 split across the world between security and insecurity of attachment style. Insecure attachments are therefore very common and not in and of themselves a cause for concern from a safeguarding perspective. We need to consider the child's attachment behaviours as adaptive strategies and use our knowledge of child development, the caregiving environment and trauma theories to make informed judgements about the welfare of any individual child. It is also important not to focus on the existence or strength of a relationship, but on the *nature* and *quality* of that relationship, as almost all children will have formed an attachment to or relationship with someone.

Attachment theory can be considered a theory of affect regulation (managing feelings), as well as of personality development in the context of caregiving relationships. Put simply, securely attached children know they can express strong feelings and articulate their needs and that they won't be rejected by their parents/caregivers as a result. This allows them to learn to effectively process affect and regulate; their parents/caregivers are giving them the message that it is okay to have big feelings and that those feelings will not overwhelm them. 'Bad as well as good times can be accessed and reflected upon

---

2   The Strange Situation procedure was designed to measure attachment behaviour in children aged 9–18 months. It looks at the balance between exploratory and attachment behaviours when the attachment figure is present, when they leave the room and upon reunion.

in measured terms. This means that individuals have the ability to deal with the world realistically without too much distortion' (Howe *et al.* 1999, p.203). When their attachment behaviours are not activated they are able to explore the world; these children can play, be curious and take risks, knowing they have a safe base to return to.

Infants are beginning to develop an *internal working model* – 'more conscious, cognitive understandings of themselves and other people' (Howe 2010, p.189) – through repeated patterns of relating with primary caregivers. If a child experiences feeling loved, loveable, valued and praised, he will come to think of himself as effective, worthy of care and of love. He will learn to anticipate how caregivers will respond when he experiences stress or need and can therefore organise strategies to maximise his feelings of security at these times. As he grows, these expectations and beliefs will guide other wider relationships too.

Some children have experienced a more challenging caregiving context where the parent/primary caregiver has been less consistently psychologically available, sensitive and responsive. 'Under these caregiving conditions, children cannot take their carer's availability for granted – hence their attachments are described as "insecure"' (Howe 2010, p.190). This child's internal working model of self and of others is likely to be less positive. He will need to develop behavioural strategies to try to keep the caregiver or parent near.

Avoidantly attached (defended) children quickly learn that their caregivers/parents prefer it if they *don't* show emotion and *don't* express needs. These children become skilled at pretending they don't have big feelings and repress or deny them when they have caregivers who 'become anxious and defensively rejecting of emotional need whenever others place demands on them' (Howe 2010, p.190). They learn that when they overtly demonstrate a need or fear through attachment behaviours, this further limits their carer's availability. So, they do their best to be very self-contained and yet are also highly sensitive to the feelings and behaviours of other people.

Where children experience abandonment, rejection, abuse or emotional harm, they can develop more extreme strategies to survive. They may not look for comfort when they're unwell, scared or distressed because they've learned that appearing to be in need can make things worse for them. They may show little distress during separation from their parent or caregiver and seem quite detached. Don't be surprised therefore if these children express few feelings in your assessment sessions or behave as if relationships are unimportant; 'using the language of emotions is likely to be frustrating and unproductive' (Schofield 1998). Superficially they may appear relatively unaffected by adverse childhood experiences. Hold in your mind, however, that this child is not avoiding relationships; he has learned that to feel safe, he must avoid closeness and shut down feelings to avoid rejection and pain.

Ambivalently attached (resistant or dependent) children tend to ramp up their emotional responses when their attachment system is activated (e.g. when they are hungry, afraid or separated from parent/caregiver). Their caregivers tend to be preoccupied with their own high emotional needs and can doubt their self-worth. They can inconsistently tune into the attachment cues or signals from their children, so the children need to develop behavioural strategies (often angry dependence, demanding, needy, provocative, pushing things 'too far') to increase the chance of their being noticed; the child learns that making persistent demands may produce a better 'strike rate'. 'They live in an unpredictable world, in which there is no guarantee that others will be there or respond at times of need or distress' (Howe 2010, p.191). This means these children can sometimes have little sense of self-efficacy or confidence that they can get their needs met by adults. They are rarely satisfied or reassured by their caregivers, and indeed can present as inconsolable on reunion.

In your assessment sessions, you may experience children who lead you to believe you are very special to them, perhaps the only one who can help. They may invite intimacy by talking openly about how difficult things are for them and how dreadfully they are treated by everyone but you. It is not unusual to see such 'splitting' where people are perceived as all *good* or all *bad*. They can be prone to sentimentalising relationships and can be very preoccupied with or obsessive about caregiving relationships, irrespective of the level of harm experienced. I have seen such presentations incorrectly described as 'strong' attachments often because of the depth of feeling when the child is separated from his caregiver.

When assessing vulnerable children and families, we should be most alert to those children with disorganised attachment behaviours when their attachment system is activated (when they have a need) because there is a strong correlation here with abuse and neglect.

This does *not* mean that every child who demonstrates disorganised attachment behaviours has been maltreated, so please avoid jumping straight to this hypothesis in your assessment. Shemmings (2016a, p.12) rationalises the research findings by defining three potential pathways to disorganised attachment behaviour:

- abusive parental behaviour – sexual or physical abuse and sometimes emotional harm and neglect

- unintentional maltreatment where caregiving is inadvertently frightening – common in mothers with post-natal depression – or where there are frequent overnight separations, extensive unplanned care (perhaps where a parent is in hospital or imprisoned) or where socio-economic and genetic risk factors combine

- no maltreatment – although it isn't clear what causes disorganised attachment behaviours they can be seen in some children with autism spectrum conditions.

In terms of assessment, there are clear parental behaviours that may lead to disorganised attachment behaviours.

- Where parents or caregivers have issues around *unresolved loss or trauma*. When caring for his infant or toddler, the parent can be reminded consciously or unconsciously of his own vulnerabilities. The child unwittingly becomes the direct cause of the parent's distress. A parental history of abuse, separation, loss and trauma can impact models of caregiving: how this parent thinks and feels about parenting his own child. Clues to this in assessment might be a parent who struggles to construct a coherent narrative of his life. He might present as emotionally labile, swinging between extremes of emotion – from cut off and dismissive to quickly overwhelmed.

- *Disconnected or insensitive caregiving*, which may include sudden changes in behaviour; parents/caregivers can present as withdrawn and neglectful of the child's needs or intrusive and aggressive in trying to meet them. Clues to this in assessment might be a *disconnected* parent who displays frightening or threatening parental behaviours, or conversely appears frightened of the child's needs and retreats from him when he sees attachment behaviours. These hostile attachment figures may threaten, menace or abuse their children and then abandon them when they express attachment needs, because this is experienced as stressful for the parent.

You might also see dissociative 'freeze' responses (see Chapter 1) like a sudden stilling of movement or changes in tone of voice. Or the parent might interact with the baby either in a very timid, submissive or helpless style or in a romanticised or sexualised manner when faced with their child's needs. Parents can sometimes switch quickly between hostile and helpless states.

An *insensitive* parent might fail to interact with the child at all and maintain a physical distance or conversely demonstrate intrusive, aggressive or harsh parental behaviours.

- *Low mentalising capacity*, which I will expand on further below. In your assessment you may perhaps observe a mother who, because she is cold herself, doesn't recognise that her baby is overdressed and overheating – she can't appreciate the baby has different feelings and intentions to her own. When you explore the parent/caregiver's own parenting history you may find he struggles to make sense of his own childhood experiences and moreover shows no curiosity about it either; for example, if you ask how he makes sense of his own parent's behaviour or actions.

Children who experience these kinds of parenting, where the parent/caregiver is the source of fear and, as the primary attachment figure, also the solution to that fear, face increased stress and anxiety.

Children try to 'escape' the source of the fear...at the same time as their activated attachment system triggers an 'approach' response to the attachment figure in the form of attachment behaviour. Behaviourally, the child finds himself or herself in an impossible situation, escape and approach behaviours are simultaneously activated. Under these conditions, children find it difficult to organise an attachment strategy that increases the carer's availability, hence the classification: disorganised attachment. (Main and Solomon, cited in Howe 2010, p.193)

The risks of children developing this style of relating is highest where: there is physical harm, sexual abuse and neglect; children are exposed to parental domestic abuse or substance misuse; there is parental depression; or there are multiple placement moves (Howe 2005). These children spend much of their energy focusing on trying to help themselves to feel safer, more secure and in control: functions of survival. They find it so hard to regulate their physiological arousal and remain for sustained periods in states of acute stress – a 'survival mode' in which it feels inordinately safer to be in control rather than to be controlled. This is because it feels impossible to trust parents/ caregivers to offer containment.

In children who have experienced such complex, developmental trauma you may observe or hear reports of some extreme behaviours or symptomology that would be indicative of significant relational difficulties. This could include:

- cruelty to animals or peers

- destructiveness

- aggression towards peers or adults

- self-injurious behaviour

- fire-setting

- issues with food – stealing and hoarding, overeating or food refusal

- issues with sleep, soiling or wetting

- lying and stealing

- sexually harmful behaviour

- superficial charm or indiscriminate affection.

Understanding mentalisation or mentalising

Mentalisation is crucial to human development, as it shapes our understanding of others and of ourselves and is central to human connection, communication and relationships. In essence, it is the capacity to see ourselves from the outside and others from the inside. The trailer to the animated film *Inside Out* gives great insight into this phenomenon. Explained simply, it is the ability to understand your own and others' mental states, as well as being able to then connect those states to feelings and behaviour. It requires accurate and detailed mindreading. 'If mentalizing is working well, thoughts are tentative and creative. There is room for humour, doubt and getting things wrong' (Thompson 2016, p.31). These are the building blocks of a secure attachment as the child develops the capacity for mentalisation through the experience of his caregivers/parents reflecting on his needs, feelings and experiences and helping him to regulate until he learns to do these things for himself. In most children, we will begin to see this between the ages of three and four.

Questions to consider when assessing a parent's or caregiver's capacity for mentalising, especially with infants and toddlers, are about his ability to 'imagine in' to the child's world. Can he hold the baby in mind? Can he tune into the baby's needs and feelings in such a way that the infant experiences safety, comfort, regulation and a feeling of being understood? Can he regulate the baby's affect, especially when he is in a state of heightened arousal (fear, distress) (Fonagy *et al.* 1998)? What does the parent think the child is thinking about him? What would this infant be saying if he could speak? Does the parent have any interest in what is in his child's mind?

Where this capacity for mentalisation goes wrong, what might you see? Parents/caregivers who:

- struggle to empathise with their child's distress or seem emotionally disconnected from it

- interpret the child's behaviour as intending to torment the parent, or attribute intention to very young infants/toddlers: 'She's trying to wind me up'

- struggle to see how the child might be experiencing the parent

- either don't mirror the child's affective states or exaggerate mirroring, which can aggravate rather than soothe the infant

- consistently misunderstand or misinterpret the child's cues, which means the parental behaviour or response is not adjusted to meet the child's needs

- lack a sense of agency or of being in control of their own behaviour or choices – things 'just happen'

- get stuck in rigid, repetitive patterns of interaction – they can struggle to consider their own and the child's behaviour from different perspective (e.g. a belief the child is refusing to eat because he knows this will upset the parent; failure to consider that the child might be full up or over-tired)

- lack playfulness or humour.

So, in the context of assessments, from an attachment or relationship-based perspective, what information will you need to gather to reach a formulation? Howe *et al.* (1999) look at 'sites of interest', which I summarise here.

Look at *factors relating to the child*: his development (physical, social, emotional, behavioural and cognitive in relation to typical developmental milestones); his relationships with brothers and sisters; his care history; peer relationships and relationships in education settings. Also look very closely at *parental/caregiver factors*: wellbeing and functioning, including their own parenting experiences and relationship history; patterns of relationships within the extended family networks; peer relationships (with friends, neighbours, colleagues); the physical environment in the home and finance; and relationships with agencies such as schools, health, social work services. You can do this through: a combination of detailed analysis of the previous history to create an integrated chronology in collaboration with other agencies; observations of the child and family in various settings; and by spending time with both the children and parents.

Howe *et al.* (1999) argue that considering all these complex factors will support you in arriving at a better understanding of: the internal working models of children and adults in the family; the quality of the caregiving system in terms of the physical, social and emotional environment; risk and protective factors (in the child and within the caregiving system); the parents' capacity to change within the child's timeframe (Brown and Ward 2013); and the support that will be required to safeguard the child.

Please also refer to the introduction to Chapter 6, which further explores the need for child-focused observation, as this is also critical to understanding the nature of relationships.

In this chapter you will find exercises to help you explore relationships within and outside the family. There will be opportunities to identify supportive social networks as well as risk factors within relationships and to understand how family members relate to and feel about each other. Please hold in mind when planning your interactions with children and young people that when a child has experienced relational trauma, he is likely to be functioning developmentally below his chronological age.

FACES TECHNIQUE

✂ Materials

A large piece of paper, pens, crayons or pencils. For children who are unable or unwilling to draw, it is useful to have some pre-prepared facial expressions, such as happy, afraid, angry, excited, sad, bored, aggressive, relaxed, etc. Young people may respond better to emojis as these are now common currency on social media and are easily downloadable for free.

✐ Process

Explain to the child that you want to learn more about his family and the people he lives with. Either show him or draw some images of different facial expressions and make sure he understands each expression and the emotion it relates to. For older or more emotionally literate children, you could use a wider range of expressions; for those at earlier stages of development, you might decide to use just two or three core emotions (e.g. happy, sad and cross).

Ask the child to draw you pictures of everyone in his family or the people he lives with and then explain that each family member needs to have just one of the facial expressions. Then ask him to choose from a range of different facial expressions and assign them to members of his family. This could be birth or foster family or people that care for him. If he says something like 'Mummy is sad and happy' ask if he can choose which one she is most like or like most often. This is a useful method for discovering how a child perceives family members or caregivers. It is more likely to appeal to younger children or those at an earlier stage of social and emotional development. You are not only looking for which expressions the child draws but also his explanation as to why – what is his thinking behind picking a particular face for one person and another face for someone else?

✓ Aims

- To help the child express feelings about family or caregivers – non-verbally if this helps.

- To consider the child's emotional literacy skills – remember if the child only chooses a very restricted range of feelings this might not be reflective of poor emotional literacy but may suggest he is very guarded or defended and doesn't want to expose any difficulties in his relationships.

- To assess the quality of the child's close relationships – how does he experience key people in his life on a feelings level?

☝ Handy hints

I have two little feelings tins; one contains cards with a vast range of feelings words (e.g. happy, miserable, disappointed, lonely, excited) and the other contains cards with a range of feelings faces. The cards are laminated so I can re-use them time and again in direct work and in training contexts. I also use the Bear Cards (Veeken, 2012) which have a tremendous range of expressions. They can be a great tool for use with anyone – child or adult – who may be finding it hard to find the words to express emotions. Just make sure that when the person chooses a feelings face, you clarify how he has interpreted that face. People who have had difficult early starts in life can sometimes have difficulty with recognising facial expressions, so don't assume the face has been interpreted in the same way you would.

This exercise is adapted from Leeds City Council's Integrated Safeguarding Unit Consultation with Children Toolkit.

QUEEN OR KING OF THE ISLAND

✂ Materials

Large A3 sheet of paper and felt tips. It is optional to bring magazines or clip-art images, but they can be useful for some people – if you do this you'll also need glue and scissors. You might also bring a small bag of miniatures (see creative toolkit in Chapter 2).

Process

On a large sheet of paper draw three islands; one large one, a smaller one next to it and a third one way down near the bottom of the page. Next draw a bridge that connects the large island to the smaller island next to it. Explain to the child that the large island is his fantasy island and that he is king of the island.

As you draw a gate at the end of the bridge, be clear that he owns the key to the gate and has the power to decide when this gate is opened or locked. Draw a key on the fantasy island. Next draw waves all around the islands and in the waves, draw sharks' fins. Put more sharks around the bottom island and some around the island adjoining the fantasy kingdom, but leave one side of this island safe for swimming.

Now hand over control of what happens on the islands to the child: who visits, who lives there and who is excluded. Begin with the fantasy island, exploring what would make it the perfect place to live. Ask which people, places or things he would want on his island *all of the time*. He can draw or write these things on the image. This could be people (Mum or best friend), places (gym club or pizza restaurant) or things (teddy, food, house).

Now consider the second island that is connected by the bridge. This island is for people or places he would like to see occasionally, but not be with all the time. Remember he has the key and so can decide when to see these people or places and when he has had enough. I would be interested in whether visitors are allowed to visit the fantasy island or does he visit them elsewhere? Again, draw these places or people on the image.

Next move to think about the third island; a place to put places or people, he never wants to see again. This is a totally secure island. People cannot travel off this island; there are no boats or planes or any means of transportation, and freezing cold shark-infested waters surround it. However, he can also choose other people or places to take their chances in shark-infested waters.

Aims

- To establish a child's feelings towards different people, relationships and places/activities.

- To understand what or who is important to him.

- To have a sense of how the child's needs are met.

✎ Handy hints

Although I have typically used this exercise with children and young people, I see no reason why this couldn't be used as an assessment tool with adults as well, especially where you understand that it might be more appropriate to engage on a creative or visual level.

Don't put limitations around what or who is placed on any island and use your curiosity to find out more about decision-making processes. Openers like 'Tell me more about…' or 'I'm wondering what…' can be helpful. I like to ask if these islands are fixed or whether anything could happen to change who lives on or has access to which island. Has it always felt this way? How about six months ago, a year, five years ago?

Where people are limited by their literacy skills, are self-conscious or lacking confidence in their drawing ability, either offer to draw/write on the image yourself or bring magazines or a selection of clip-art images to choose from. If you have a bag of miniatures in your toolkit, there is no reason why you couldn't offer the option of choosing objects to represent people or places to put them on the island. Like the Sculpting exercise in Chapter 5, this gives you the option of physically moving the objects from island to island to imagine in to how it might feel.

I'm unsure of the origin of this exercise. Thanks to Athaliah Durrant for her work on this. I have also found a similar version on the Durham Local Safeguarding Children Board website (www.durham-lscb.org.uk).

RELATIONSHIPS: OKAY, DIFFICULT, WRONG

✂ Materials

Three boxes with labels – OKAY, DIFFICULT and WRONG, and pre-printed cards with different kinds of relationships on them. Have at least 30 permutations and tailor them according to the individual needs and experiences of the child and family. Categorise the relationships, for example, into:

Friendly relationship between

a group of 14-year-old boys

two girls aged 16

a girl aged 14 and male care officer in her children's home

girl aged 15 and the taxi driver who takes her to school

boy aged 17 with a learning disability and a male neighbour aged 23

Lasting relationship between

mother and daughter aged 11

uncle and nephew aged 14

boy aged 17 and his female foster carer

boy and girl aged 18

male teacher aged 43 and female pupil aged 14 after she moves to a new school

babysitter aged 21 and child aged 7

Loving/sexual/intimate relationship between

an unmarried man and woman

adult man and boy aged 16

a child and an adult

girl aged 14 and boy aged 19

two married adult women

two willing adults of any age and gender

boy aged 18 and his female teacher at college

a seven-year-old boy and his mother

a 17-year-old girl with physical disabilities and her personal assistant

Process

This is an exercise developed by the NSPCC (1997), which can be used in groups or with individuals. In a family or sibling group, individuals can read out and discuss cards before making a decision about which box to consign the card to, but in an individual assessment session, the parent, child or the young person can explore his thinking with the worker. You can use this exercise to consider the nature of relationships and how different people might express their friendship, love or care for another. You might explore how this differs in different cultures or countries.

Think about the differences between a loving family relationship and an intimate relationship in terms of the expression of physical affection and love. Is a sexual relationship always connected with being 'in love'? Where you are concerned about possible sexual exploitation or sexual harm, especially where the child may not recognise the relationship as abusive, you can also think about definitions of consent and what informed consent is and isn't. The legal context is important here, so be sure to have up-to-date knowledge in this area.

Aims

– To explore different kinds of relationships and to distinguish between okay, difficult and wrong relationships.

– To allow for conversations about abusive relationships, even where it is not perceived to be so.

Handy hints

You can develop endless permutations on different relationship cards, including cross-cultural relationships or relationships for people with disabilities or additional needs.

OUR STREET OR OUR COMMUNITY

Materials

Card house templates or different-sized cardboard boxes, trays and paint.

 Process

This is an adaptation of an exercise by Tait and Wosu (2016). They suggest it is done in the early or initial assessment phase over two or three sessions. They invite the parent and/or children to recreate the street or community in which they live, using a variety of different-sized and shaped cardboard boxes, which are held in cardboard trays (the kind you can pick up sometimes in supermarkets that have held tins or fresh fruit). They spend one session creating the scene, the next painting/decorating the scene and the third playing with the model.

A quicker alternative would be to create the scene using cardboard/paper house templates (which can still be drawn on or decorated) to explore how the family defines its place in the community or the street they live in. This could therefore extend to recreational areas, shops and local amenities or school. Families might, for example, identify with a particular block of flats, housing estate or community centre. You can use this period of creativity to have conversations about the nature of the community:

Is it a source of support or stress?

Is the family connected with other local people or scapegoated?

Do extended family members live nearby? Are they supportive? In what way, yes or no?

Are particular members of the family more isolated than others?

Is there a sense of community cohesion?

Does it feel like a safe space to live?

✓ Aims

- To understand a child and family in the context of the community in which they live.

- To explore how the family defines their world.

- To identify wider sources of family support.

- To assess whether the family is socially isolated or can access support locally.

☝ Handy hints

This activity connects well the principle of looking for strengths within family systems and of families identifying their own solutions. Remember that a common pitfall in assessments is insufficient full engagement with parents, especially fathers, but also with extended family members, to be able to assess risk (Broadhurst et al. 2010). This activity can help you identify key figures in the family ecology.

You will find that when working with a family group, it will often be the children who lead and adults who follow and eventually join the fun. If you extend the activity across several sessions and reach the point where you can play and interact with the model – for example encouraging each family member to tell a story, either real or from their imagination using the model – you may gain insight into what life looks like for the child/parent or how he would like it to be in the future. You can be curious about the model – is there anything he would change? Is there anyone he would like to invite into the scene or conversely keep out? If you have your bag of miniatures with you (see creative toolkit in Chapter 2), you could use these to interact with the community or street scene too.

BUTTONS AND BEADS

✂ Materials

A selection of beads or buttons and something to thread them onto – this could be yarn or string or if you are making jewellery you will need nylon, leather or beading thread.

✎ Process

This is an adaptation of Tait and Wosu's (2013) activity called Beads and Badges. Ask the child if he would prefer buttons or beads (if you have both on offer) and then whether he would prefer to make a bracelet or necklace or just a chain.

You can spend some time looking through the beads or buttons, seeing which he is drawn to and wondering why. He can thread as many as he likes, but for each bead he has to name someone he knows. With a good selection on offer, you should be able to think about the reasons why a particular bead or button is chosen for a particular person. You might need to offer gentle prompts: which bead could you choose for your dad, your teacher, your childminder, your neighbour, etc.

Once the chain is made, you can celebrate how wonderful it looks and how special the child is to have so many connections and important people in his life. Think about whom he'd like to share it with? Perhaps with some of the people represented on the bracelet or chain?

✓ Aims

– To help you identify people with whom the child is connected.

– To think about possible support networks or safe adults who could build resilience.

👍 Handy hints

Tait and Wosu (2013) helpfully suggest you can buy old necklaces in charity shops or car boot sales and dismantle them for use in this activity. This would potentially be a cheaper option, but you can also buy child-friendly beads in most toy and craft/hobby shops.

Make sure you keep a note of who was put on the chain and the associations with that person if they emerge.

THE EMPTY CHAIR

✂ Materials

None.

✏ Process

Oaklander (1988, p.152) describes this technique, originally developed by Fritz Perls, a psychoanalyst who was one of the founders of Gestalt therapy, as a way of converting 'past, unresolved situations into present, focused experience'. When working with a parent/carer or older young person to explore relationships, ask him to imagine someone (himself, a relative or part of himself, e.g. the angry part or the overeating part) is sitting in a nearby chair. Rather than talking to the practitioner directly about the issues in the relationship, for example with a deceased or absent parent or with a tricky adolescent, encourage the individual to talk to the chair – to imagine telling the person what he would be telling the practitioner.

This is a simple approach that can help work through or explore internal or interpersonal struggles or conflicts. Role-play can help individuals to see a situation from a different perspective and gain insight into feelings or behaviours. Simply put, you encourage reflection on what the world might look like from another's eyes. The individual begins by talking to the 'empty chair' explaining his thoughts or feelings. He is then encouraged to sit on the chair himself, assuming the role of the other person or part of himself (such as his rage or guilt) and respond to what has just been said. He may move back and forth from chair to chair a number of times throughout the dialogue.

✓ Aims

- To bring unfinished situations or conversations into the here and now.

- To bring greater awareness of and clarity to complex relationships.

- To help the child/parent understand his feelings about himself or a significant other.

- To help the child/parent view a conflict or conflictual relationships from a different perspective – and potentially gain insight into why he feels or behaves in a particular way.

☝ Handy hints

You might use this technique if you recognise a specific conflict within the family system or within an individual that may benefit from further exploration. It can help an individual to connect with a feeling, an idea or aspect of his personality that he has tried to ignore or deny; in this way we can help people accept that conflicts exist within us all.

If you are working with a parent and child together they can role-play and physically swap seats; the parent will take the role of the child and vice versa. Using masks or puppets can sometimes help free children and young people up to authentically say what they think and feel.

CHAPTER 5

HEARING THE FAMILY STORIES

In our work with vulnerable children and families, we cannot disregard what has come before, even when faced with a crisis in the here and now. Some families experience multiple and complex difficulties, which are often intergenerational and likely to impact on outcomes for children. We need to 'examine family difficulties in a wide context, rather than focusing on investigating single events' which are unlikely to capture the complexity of family dynamics (Devine 2015, p.7). Families are living systems, and we should be looking at the difficulties within systems of relationships: promoting change within the broader system rather than simply within individuals. The interconnectedness of families, groups, organisations and inter-professional relationships means that an action in one part of the system can invoke a significant reaction in another part of the system. All parts of a family are interrelated, and no part can be understood fully in isolation from the rest of the system (Walker 2012). The telling of family stories and experiences should play a key role in understanding what is happening in a family in the here and now. It is vital that we look at wider family, including significant others identified by the nuclear family, especially non-resident parents.

One of the three domains in the *Framework for the Assessment of Children in Need and their Families* (DoH 2000) is family and environmental factors, including:

- community resources
- family's social integration

- income

- employment

- housing

- wider family

- family history and functioning.

This chapter will focus on the assessment of family history and functioning, the wider family and social integration and how these impact on a child's development and on parenting capacity. Any understanding of a child must be located within the context of that child's family, community and the culture in which he is being raised (DoH 2000). In the absence of any better indicator, often the best guide to future behaviour is past behaviour; yet this is an area to which practitioners have historically at times given too little weight. If we fail fully to explore the parent/caregiver's own histories, we miss opportunities to notice intergenerational patterns of relating or family stories that will help inform our judgements about what might be happening currently. It is also important of course to consider whether this is how the family would typically function, or whether this is how it functions in the context of particular stressors.

The family life cycle is critical; it identifies tasks that different family members have to negotiate at different times in their life; it's a window into the developmental needs of everyone within the family. Moving from one life stage to another brings challenges, and it is often around such transitions that families encounter difficulties. For example, this could be the birth of a new baby, or an older child moving into adolescence or out of the family home to live independently. In this dimension, children's needs are more likely to be met if they have a stable home life, with consistent caregivers and opportunities to socialise, and have relationships with family and peers. It is important to consider the stability and endurance of familial bonds and whether individuals within the nuclear and extended family system feel a sense of belonging to people who matter to them and to whom they matter.

Families don't exist in a vacuum, and to understand how they function we must use all available evidence to build a comprehensive picture, without sole reliance on practice knowledge or past predictive behaviour in isolation. It is important to liaise with other agencies in relation to family and environmental factors such as housing services, the police, youth workers or religious leaders. They may support you to gain insight into particular influences on the child or his parents/ caregivers and to verify facts and opinions shared during the assessment sessions. Gilligan (2010) talks about critical relationships between children and caregivers, including adult children and their parents, which we hope would be protective influences. He also discusses the important protective role of non-parental adults 'with a strong and ideally partisan commitment to the child' such as extended family, a friend's parents, teachers or sports coaches and community leaders. This gains more significance when relationships with primary caregivers are compromised; children have more need of other compensatory relationships.

Holland (2010, p.111) reminds us that exploration of family stories and experiences is

> not a neutral process. It is also an intervention. By asking people to consider such personal aspects of their lives, practitioners may cause them to reflect, acknowledge difficulties they may have faced (or even caused others to face in cases of domestic violence or child abuse) and even think and act differently about their lives.

We must anticipate that this may be a challenge, especially in the context of trauma histories. We must approach this work from a position of first believing the family is the expert in its own experiences and can also therefore contribute to finding its own solutions to difficulties.

> A family's structure and organisation will determine to some degree what is possible within that particular family. There is no 'normal' family structure. The question therefore must be 'Does this structure work for this family? And further does it allow for the healthy growth of family members?' (Walker 2012, p.5)

Don't overlook the impact of 'culture and ethnicity as crucial influences on the interactional style and structure of families.... We cannot make assumptions about the internal structure of a family from their known culture, as defined by crude stereotypes or lazy generalisations, since there will always be individual interpretations in any culture or religion and we need to take the time to reflect upon and understand these' (Walker 2012, pp.16–17).

Observations of family exchanges during the activities that follow in this chapter also help inform your assessment. Note behaviour and affect expressed between children and their adult caregivers, siblings and parents, including the feel and tone of interactions within the family units. You should be mindful of the quality of relationships between parents/caregivers and each individual child, as parents may be able to meet the needs of one child but not another.

> It is important to note how the family interacts, in particular being vigilant to signs of family disunity, poor communication, inflexibility and animosity between the adults – these features of family functioning are strong indicators of a number of different types of child maltreatment. (NSPCC 2015, p.5)

These activities will support you in considering how well connected the family is to other systems or community resources. You will learn whether children and families have access to supportive relationships within the family and within their social network. You will explore the parent's experiences as a child and identify any positive perceptions or memories of their own childhood in relation to his role as a parent in the present. This necessitates the construction of a family history, including experiences of previous involvement with support services and outcomes of this for the child.

GENOGRAM OR FAMILY TREE

✂ Materials
Pens and paper – A4 and A3 sized. It is optional to have a selection of feelings faces too.

✎ Process
Genograms have long been used in work with children and families with multiple functions, but primarily to achieve a graphic representation of family members and their relationships, preferably over at least three generations. You can draw them with parents/caregivers or with children and young people, which can be helpful in clarifying issues for both parties. While there are conventions for drawing genograms, which you must follow for court reports (see Handy hints), in a direct work activity, especially with a child, there is no need to be so prescriptive.

Begin by asking whether you should draw the family tree or does the individual want to do the writing. You can have a selection of different shapes to choose from (which can be easily created in Word or other computer programs, then printed and cut out) or you can stick with convention.

You would usually begin by adding the person you're making the family tree with, but could equally simply ask, 'Tell me about who is in your family.' If this is tricky, then after adding the service user, then move to their parents' names, age or date of birth, and date or cause of death if applicable. If either parent has been married more than once, get information about those relationships too. Then ask for siblings' details, beginning with the eldest on the left. If the person has been married or was in previous significant relationships, next add these details, together with their children in birth order. If these children are married, add information about their spouses and children if appropriate. Finally, ask if there are any non-relatives who are very important or 'like family'. Remember that you should be concerned as much with perceptions of who represents 'family' as much as who is technically family.

This activity is useful for looking at how families change, and who comes in and out of someone's life. I always like to ask if there is someone who used to be part of the family, but isn't currently on the family tree. Maybe he could choose an alternative symbol for this person. Conversely, is there someone who is on the picture who he would prefer not to be? Again, an alternative symbol can be chosen to represent someone he would like to be missing. As with the Sculpting exercise later in this chapter, it can be useful to extend this activity to understand a person's emotional connection to people on the genogram. You can have feelings faces or emojis ready to attach to individuals and then ask if he can recall a time when the person presented this way.

Remember, don't just record the facts; as you construct the image, take the opportunity to have a conversation about family relationships. Who does he go to if he is upset? Who gets on best with whom? Who does he have the most fun with? Who is the 'good one' and who gets in trouble the most? Can he think of three words to describe his mum, grandad, brother, cousin, etc.?

You can also ask hypothetical questions and write on speech bubbles to give the imagined replies – for example, 'What do you think X likes most about you?'

It may also be possible to gather other information about any difficulties within the family system. Which family members know about the problem(s)? How do others perceive it? Has anyone offered any solutions or support? Has anyone in the family had similar issues, for example, with offending behaviour, drug or alcohol misuse, mental health?

Cultural genograms allow exploration of themes within the family system and family life cycle, which could relate to geographic location, historical or cultural factors. This encourages discussion around patterns of relating, intergenerational transmission of trauma, and an understanding of how the family or an individual in the family system is positioned. As well as commonalities you will also find areas of difference emerge if you sensitively explore issues around gender, sexuality, class, spirituality, race, education, mental health, values and beliefs, and so on (Treisman 2017).

✓ Aims

- To elicit information about family composition and perceptions of the family composition; a quick visual representation of the complexity of a family system.

- To explore and clarify family relationships and dynamics – who can be available to provide support?

- To identify intergenerational patterns of relating and make visible life-cycle issues; what happened in one generation will often repeat itself in the next.

- To look at how this family might have changed over time and who has come in and out. These complicated relationships can be an additional stressor for children because the changes can be difficult for them to comprehend.

- To identify any significant history or patterns of behaviour that may be relevant to an individual's medical or psychological functioning.

☝ **Handy hints**

For the purposes of assessment there is no absolute right or wrong way to construct a genogram. However, if you are *not* following convention, make sure you make a note of the meaning of the symbols or shapes you utilise.

Where family structures are complicated or extensive, the picture you draw can soon look messy and can be hard to contain on one small piece of paper; consider using lining paper, which offers you more scope and freedom. You can always re-write it more neatly later or construct a diagram on the computer. Although some local authority recording systems can generate genograms for you, this is not a reason to avoid this exercise. The idea is rather to offer the child, parent or family the opportunity to share information that is important to them, as well as creating opportunities for noticing emerging patterns of relating that will inform your understanding of the family script.

There are a few basic premises in drawing a traditional genogram. The male is always at the left of the family, female on the right. A spouse must be closer to his/her first partner than to the second/third partner, etc. Children are listed in birth order with the eldest child always on the left and the youngest at the right of the family. Birth date or age is written above if you have it. Age at death is written inside the symbol and date of death on the right above (e.g. 1967–1992).

You can also represent who lives together in different households by drawing a dashed (- - - -) circle around people who live in the same house.

This is of course a far from exhaustive list and free guides to creating genograms are easily found online. Above all, please be mindful of the considerable, if unintended, impact of some symbols. The use of the cross to symbolise death of a family member may be one such example. Also, be sensitive to how the individual identifies in terms of gender and sexuality.

□	Male
○	Female
△	Unknown gender
▣	Transgender man to woman
◎	Transgender woman to man
▽	Gay male
⊖	Lesbian
⬯	Bisexual
⊠	Miscarriage/termination
✖	Death
◇	Pet
▲	Family secret

Figure 5.1 Typical genogram symbols, based on those
used by the Multicultural Family Institute

DRAW YOUR FAMILY

✂ Materials

Paper, pens/pencils/paint (other collage materials such as fabric, coloured paper, scissors – optional).

✐ Process

Ask the child (or parent/carer) to draw his family, including himself, doing something together. Some children might need a little prompting to think of a scenario to draw. You might suggest depicting a day out, a teatime or a special celebration. Encourage the child to draw his picture any way he likes and to include whomever he feels to be part of the family. Pets often feature here, as might neighbours or family friends.

Explore the image with the child, asking who the figures are and what they are doing. It might then be possible to discuss the child's feelings about family members and his perceptions of relationships between people. You might encourage individuals on the picture to 'talk to each other' or you could add speech bubbles. Above all, show interest and curiosity to learn more about the child and his family.

It is interesting to see who the child puts on his picture and who is excluded. When doing this activity with a child in care, notice whether he draws only his birth family or whether the foster family is also present. Is the family doing something together or are members more isolated? Who is drawn close to whom? And do the child's descriptions of people fit with their representations on the paper? (Wrench and Naylor 2013).

✓ Aims

- To assess the child's view of his family and whom he considers to be part of the family.

- To find out more about where the child places himself in relation to other family members.

- To open up discussion with the child about family life and unearth stories and anecdotes relating to their experiences in their family. Anecdotes are often positive for the child, no matter how insignificant they might seem to us.

👍 Handy hints

This activity is particularly useful for children who struggle with language, as their picture can tell a story very eloquently without the need for long verbal explanations.

There is no reason why you shouldn't do this activity either with parents/caregivers separately or with a family group as both would give alternative perspectives on the family script. Another option working with a parent/carer is to ask him to draw himself as a child doing something he used to enjoy. Suggest he try to identify the feelings he would have experienced at the time and now looking back. This simple activity can be so useful in terms of opening up discussion about his own childhood experiences. Is this image of him alone or with friends or family? Can he draw on a positive memory? Many carers I have asked to share a funny or positive story from their school days have struggled to identify anything positive at all.

ECOMAP

Materials

Paper and pens.

Process

This exercise is similar to Sculpting (see later in this chapter) and can be done with children or adults with nothing more than a pen and paper. Adults and children can benefit from an approach that is more visual than verbal, especially if: they are feeling negative or defensive about the assessment process; they have a learning disability and benefit from visual prompts; they are struggling to process thoughts and feelings and might be helped by visually mapping this out.

Explain you would like some help with constructing a picture of his and his family's important relationships; or what makes his world. Ask the individual to place himself in a circle in the middle of the paper and begin with his household. Then ask him to identify important people or organisations (e.g. school, GP, support group) in his life and draw circles to contain them as necessary. It can help to organise thinking if you start with the household, extended family then environmental systems. Other environmental systems may be identified in relation to previous history or possible future involvement.

Draw lines between the circles where connections exist using specific lines to indicate the nature or quality of that link. You will find that people use different lines to represent different connections so make sure you are consistent and that you include a key. You can use arrowheads (→) to indicate the direction of influence, energy or resources for each relationship. For example, an arrow pointing to the client from the system would suggest the system primarily influences the client and vice versa. In some cases, there will be a two-directional flow. The ecomap has the potential for identifying strengths and needs, as well as past or present reciprocation.

_____   strong or positive connection

--------   weak or tenuous connection

....   stressful relationship

A stressful relationship can often also be represented as a line with crosses through, a wavy line or + + + + + + + + +.

Figure 5.2 Representing the strength of relationships

The distance of the circle from the individual could represent physical or emotional distance, so be sure to clarify this. You might also offer the option of using different colours to represent different feelings – positive or negative – towards different parts of the system. You could also offer feelings, faces or photos as symbols to use alongside the words. Leave any omissions of people you deem to be significant, which are certainly common when working this way with children and young people, until the end of the activity as they are rarely 'forgotten' and are usually a message to you.

As an extension to this activity you could ask the individual to reconfigure the ecomap in the way he would like it to be. This is interesting, especially with parents/caregivers, as it offers the opportunity to assess capacity for change; does he see the system as broken beyond repair, or identify hopeful possibilities moving forward? Sometimes seeing a tangible representation of what might be possible can help people envisage it in reality and think about the steps to change, even where a situation might seem very stuck.

Fahlberg (1991) suggests creating an ecomap worksheet for the child to complete the information blanks. Figure 5.3 shows a simple adaptation of such a worksheet, but you could be much more creative. You should have the child's name, age and date at the top, but then can adjust the areas of concern or strengths as appropriate.

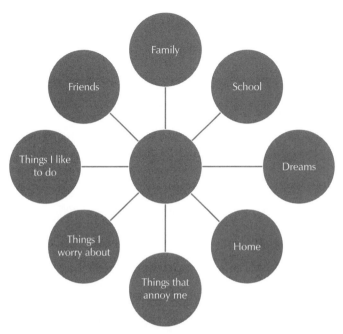

Figure 5.3 Child's ecomap

✓ Aims

- To create a visual representation of the present family system as seen by individuals within it, in relation to the external world.

- To explore with the individual to whom he feels emotionally connected and establish the value placed on relationships with others – both individuals and organisations and not just in the family system. What resources, if any, do they exchange?

- To learn about people or connections you may not have been aware of but are important to the individual, as well as identifying people who are omitted from the ecomap and if possible the reasons why.

- To view the system or ecology around the child, noticing both the strengths perspective as well as focusing on problem areas.

- To identify the extent of support systems – in friends, neighbours, clubs, professional agencies, third sector organisations and social or religious groups.

– To assess whether the boundaries between the family and their environment are open or closed. Boundary questions to ask might be:

Is this family open to new experiences or relationships?

To what extent might it be closed?

Can family members make relationships with other people and organisations outside of the family unit?

Does this family protect its members when necessary?

Does this family allow others 'in' emotionally or physically?

☝ Handy hints

Don't forget to date your ecomap. It can be a useful document to return to as, over time, relationships may shift and change and you may wish to re-evaluate or re-map. This can be a great way to look at whether there have been increased levels of social and family connectedness and more or less reliance on professional services. You can also see whether services are being duplicated or whether there is effective communication between agencies providing those services.

Carefully consider the way you explain the process, as some will assume that by 'close' you mean physically close in distance rather than emotionally close, both of which are of course relevant. You might want to suggest that he thinks of people or support services that are important to him.

If appropriate you might show the finished ecomap to other family members to help them gain insight into how the person views his family network. This can be much more powerful than a verbal description to aid understanding or reflection.

LIFE GRAPH OR LIFE MAP

✂ Materials

Large drawing paper or a roll of lining paper and pens/crayons (optional – photos, magazines, craft materials, clip-art images suitable for the theme).

Process

This activity can be done with children, caregivers or a family group to build a timeline of events from birth to the present. To explain the process, I'll focus on engaging the child, who you will support to design an image that represents his life story, reflecting his experiences – both highs and lows – and different life stages. He can write dates, names, places, etc., or use pictures, photographs or symbols to illustrate the story. Remember to let the child go at his pace; however frustrating for you, he is unlikely to recall events in chronological order.

Resist the temptation to add information yourself initially or to make corrections where you feel the child has been mistaken. This is an opportunity to identify any misconceptions or misunderstandings the child may have about his story. You will learn where gaps later need to be filled or distorted thinking corrected (e.g. where he might take responsibility for adult behaviour). Don't feel you must complete the life map in one session – it can be helpful to return to it as your relationship develops and the child has more confidence in you.

The image can be as creative or simple as you choose but often by theming the activity to respond to the child's special interests you will increase engagement. For example, for a young child who likes playing with cars you could make a road map image, using road signs and markings to enhance the story. If during the session you begin to develop a hypothesis about this child's or family's experience, be sure to check it out. 'I've noticed...' or 'I've been wondering about... What do you think?' Has anything surprised him about his image? Does any event or time strike him as significant?

Aims

- To gain understanding of a child's or family's journey and events from the family perspective (even if you hold information in a chronology or because of previous involvement, you may not be fully aware of the family story).

- To assess the individual's position and understanding of his story. You will potentially learn as much by looking at what is missing from the image as by noticing what is included.

– To explore successes and accomplishments in life as well as any difficulties he has experienced along the way. In this way you will have the opportunity to boost resilience and confidence, and the story will not be entirely problem saturated.

– To assess who shared times of trauma or upset – interruptions in parenting or moves, etc.

☞ Handy hints

This activity can be used with an adult family member to gain perspective on his past experiences. Notice whether he can share a coherent narrative account of his life. Do you see intergenerational patterns of relating emerging? Are past mistakes repeated or does the individual appear to learn or move on? In families where there has been multi-generational abuse, have parents come to over-identify with their own child's trauma? Do caregivers hold beliefs stemming from their own birth families that are unhelpful to their children?

This exercise can support you when obtaining a family history to 'look for overall patterns, expectations, strengths and weaknesses' (Fahlberg 1991, p.236). Use this activity alongside others such as the ecomap and genogram but remember it may not be possible to complete it in one session. It is important not to set someone up to talk about difficult issues then close them down because you're out of time. Similarly, if the person whizzes through the exercise and renders it entirely factual, don't labour the point. Perhaps it is too difficult to talk about what has happened or there is not yet enough safety in your relationship.

You can develop this exercise into a family timeline to correlate the impact of significant events on different family members in relation to their age and stage of development. For example, considering the impact of maternal drug use on an unborn baby or on a five-year-old child or the impact of a house move out of area for an adolescent taking his GCSEs next year.

What happens to the life map at the end is important too, and you will need to be explicit at the beginning about whether you will keep it, photograph it or leave it with the family until next time – maybe they might want to add to it and share it when you next meet. Don't underestimate the potential impact or power of seeing a life mapped out in this visual way. Even something as seemingly simple as illustrating house or school moves can be reminders of difficult or traumatic events for family members and should therefore be explored with compassion and sensitivity.

SCULPTING

✂ Materials

A variety of objects, which could include small figures of people and animals, or objects like buttons, pebbles, shells or pine cones; pretty much anything you can carry in a small bag or box to a session. Large piece of paper and pen.

🖊 Process

This exercise is a more creative version of the Ecomap activity (earlier in this chapter) and can be done with children or adults. You will support the individual to create a three-dimensional representation of his family and systemic network, noticing both space and distance as the objects are placed. The exercise can reveal feelings, bonds, conflicts, hostility and isolation or scapegoating as the family structure is revealed.

For simplicity of explanation, I'll assume you are working with a child. Ask him to choose an object to represent himself. Try to avoid giving too much direction so that you invite creativity and initiative. You can then explore why he has chosen a certain item; he may have a clear reason or it may just have caught his eye. Ask him to place it on a large piece of paper and then suggest he creates his own world around it, choosing objects for important people in his life. This might include family, friends, pets, people he lives with, people he doesn't see or even people who have died. Leave any omissions of people you consider significant, which are certainly common when working this way with children and young people, until the end of the sculpt as they are rarely 'forgotten' and are usually a message to you.

Allow the child to place each object in relation to himself on the sculpt, considering how close/connected or not he feels to the person. Explore whom each object represents and the reasons it was chosen. You might then ask him to describe the person to you using a couple of adjectives. I find it helpful to draw around each object on the paper and write down any words the child uses to describe people, so that the picture is not lost when the sculpt is dismantled. Children often like you to do the writing for them – but ask first, don't assume. You might also like to take a photo of the sculpt as an aide memoire before it is de-constructed at the end of the session.

As an extension to this activity, you could ask the person to reconfigure the sculpt in the way he would like or prefer it to be. This is interesting, especially with parents/caregivers, as it offers the opportunity to assess capacity for change; does he see the system as broken beyond repair, or can he identify hopeful possibilities moving forward? Sometimes seeing a tangible representation of what might be possible can help people envisage it in reality and think about the steps to change, even where a situation might seem very stuck.

An alternative to total reconfiguration is to experiment with moving the objects on the sculpt either closer to the child – 'What would X need to do to move closer?' – or further away – 'Are there any times when X feels more distant or disconnected?' You can represent these movements with arrows on the sculpt. Then investigate what it feels like to have X closer, etc. For example, if you move a figure closer to the child's object on the sculpt, you might ask, 'How does it feel to have X close by?'

✓ Aims

- To create a visual representation of the present family system as seen by those within it.

- To explore with the individual those whom he feels emotionally close to and establish the value he places on his relationships with others.

- To learn something about the individual's sense of self and how he views others by what objects he chooses to represent them.

- To learn about people you may not have been aware of, but who are important to the child/parent.

- To identify which people are omitted from the sculpt and if possible the reasons why.

- To view the family system as a whole, noticing both the strengths perspective as well as focusing on problem areas.

Handy hints

Think carefully about the number of objects you present to a child for this exercise. It is easy to overwhelm very young or uncontained children with too much choice.

Also consider the way you explain the process as some will assume that by close you mean physically close in distance rather than emotionally close. You might want to suggest that he thinks of people that are important to him.

If appropriate you could show the finished sculpt to other family members as this might help to gain insight into how the individual views his family network. This can be much more powerful than a verbal description.

STORY IN A BOX

Materials

An attractive-looking box (or boxes) containing small figures or objects – you must include miniatures that could represent a family (people or animals) and objects or figures that could represent the following:

Home: house, bed, cooker

Travel: boat, car, train

Fear/worry: monster, big spider, dinosaur

Friend: dog, beanie baby, small soft toy

Treasure: gemstone, costume jewellery, coins

Adventure: rope, pebble, key, mini torch.

Process

This simple exercise can make use of some of the miniatures you have in your toolkit (see Chapter 2) and is a good opportunity to assess multiple aspects of a child's presentation and internal world. It's a good alternative to the Six-Part Story exercise (Chapter 6) and more suited perhaps to younger children.

You will share the box with the child – or if you have several boxes made up, allow him to look inside and choose the one he is most drawn to – and invite him to create a story using the contents of the box. He can choose whether to use all or just one of the objects or simply the box. The development of the story is also the child's choice; you will find sometimes he will replay a familiar story, or something he has watched on TV. Other children will offer you a glimpse into their own family stories; remember, play is a powerful means of communication of unconscious processes.

Only intervene if the child seems stuck or doesn't know where to begin. Then you might offer gentle starter prompts to stimulate his imagination. For example, 'I wonder who this is?', 'What could this monster be called?', 'If these two characters met, what do you think might happen?' Help him to set the scene. 'What time of day is it?', 'Where are they?', 'What does the landscape look like?', 'What can he see, smell, hear?'

Make sure you give sufficient time warning for the story to reach its conclusion. Be mindful that not all children will end the story well and you need to accept and acknowledge this. Once the story is complete try to make a record of what the child has produced. This may be by taking a photograph of the final scene or, if you have time, making an image or writing the story down (you or the child can do this).

✓ Aims

- To observe free play – can the child use the objects to play imaginatively?

- To assess the child's developmental stage in relation to play and social interaction.

- To observe the child in interactions with his environment, including you – are you invited to join the play? Does he ask for your help? Is there shared engagement or enjoyment of the task?

– To observe themes in the play as this may gain you access to the child's internal world *and* his lived experience.

Handy hints

By using stories and toys, you offer a child or young person an alternative means of communication that, for some, can feel safer than verbal communication, especially where children have had no voice or have been silenced. He can express his own thoughts and feelings in a 'one step removed' way or through metaphor. Just be careful in this exercise not to overlay your own interpretation of events onto the child's story. Remain curious and wondering, and don't make assumptions that he is literally representing his own world. It is more helpful to validate and respond to the feelings the child expresses through play.

This can be used as a one-off session, but equally if you have more time, you can revisit the story in future sessions. You may find that the same story is repetitively replayed or that the child would like to alter the story, perhaps by changing the ending or creating an entirely new narrative.

CHAPTER 6

EXPLORING EVERYDAY LIVED EXPERIENCE

Understanding the experience of a child or young person and, crucially for assessment purposes, then making sense of wishes and feelings about his life is a far from straightforward process. Listening to a child is more complex than simply hearing his view about what he would like to happen, where he would like to live or the quality of his relationships with caregivers. Indeed, sometimes if we only listen to what is said, we risk being lulled into a state of false reassurance that all is well within a family.

'Children and young people, like adults, value the relational aspects of social work intervention' (Holland 2010, p.116), so aim to involve them as soon as possible in the assessment to allow for a relationship to develop over time. This includes ensuring, in an age-appropriate way, that the child is aware of your role and responsibilities and understands the process and purpose of the assessment. When delivering training, we encourage social workers to spend time practising writing to a child to explain precisely this.

Although it is widely accepted that it is good practice to ensure and enable children's participation in assessments, we need to go beyond 'seeing' the child and recording this as a tick box activity in case recordings. Rather, this concept of 'seeing' must be expanded to report on how the child looked, moved, smelt and interacted with you and with any others present, especially parents/caregivers, as well as the physical environment in which he was 'seen'. Without integrating the child's perspective on his life into your analysis, any assessment will be incomplete yet Serious Case Reviews continue to identify repeated failures to do so effectively. Munro (2011, p.25) summarises the primary issues, which include:

- not seeing children enough or not actively seeking their views or feelings

- failure to assimilate information from adults who try to speak for the child

- caregivers actively working to prevent workers from having direct access to the child – so the child remains unseen and unheard

- over-focus on adult rather than child needs – or what the adult risks and needs mean for the daily life of the child

- poor analysis and interpretation of evidence that would enable protection of the child.

The creative ideas you'll find in this chapter will support you to engage more meaningfully with children, but it is also worth holding in mind the potential barriers children face in sharing their experiences, their wishes and feelings about their lives. Dalzell and Sawyer (2016, pp.104–105) summarise the research findings for children, which included complaints about not seeing workers enough or not seeing them alone, which significantly limited the children's opportunities for sharing information. Other factors included:

- lack of awareness that the behaviour was abusive

- shame, embarrassment and self-blame

- stigma, loss of credibility, friends finding out

- the fear of loss of control and of people taking over

- getting someone else into trouble or splitting the family up

- loyalty to or feeling sorry for the abuser

- access to someone to tell, not knowing where to go for help

- concerns about confidentiality

- concerns about whether the person is competent to deal with the issue

- fear that telling will make things worse and that the abuser will be told that they have disclosed

- not being able to express themselves

- believing in self-reliance, not wishing to burden others.

So, when you are beginning to think about how to work with children to understand what a day in their life looks like, you will need to bear these restraining factors in mind, as well as listening to what young people say is more helpful or supportive. Be empathic about and validate the struggle to share information; it can feel scary, especially if the child is anxious about the nature of your involvement. Children report that it can help if: they have a choice about where to meet: you keep in touch between sessions; you help to sort out problems; you get them involved in activities; and you are positive and fun (Dalzell and Sawyer 2016).

As well as in formal direct work activities, it is possible to gain understanding of family life informally through observation during the assessment, even when it's not your primary focus for the session. Horwath (2010, p.67) stresses the need to be transparent about this with families at the beginning of the assessment, 'especially if factors such as cultural or religious diversity may influence what is being observed and its possible interpretation'. It isn't acceptable for families to be unaware that these informal observations, for example about the physical condition of the home or parent–child interactions, will be recorded and become part of the information spine. It is also imperative in every formal observation that the parent/carer is aware why the observation is taking place, consents to it and that there is recognition that contrived contexts for observation can influence behaviour (Holland 2004).

Observing children and young people and their caregivers

One of the prime pitfalls in assessment is a failing to see the child as an individual, not just in terms of his relationships and development. A lack of child observational data in reports and assessments can result in workers 'missing vital clues about wellbeing and safety' (Broadhurst *et al.* 2010, p.18). Assessments ought to include detailed and qualitative observations that give insight to the child's lived experience. This is especially important for more vulnerable groups such as infants and toddlers who are non-verbal or unable to tell you what life is like for them, or for children with physical or learning difficulties, deaf children and children who don't speak English as a first language. It is also important to recognise the challenges inherent in observing and spending time with 'invisible' or elusive adolescents who may choose not to be at home when you visit or to stay hidden away upstairs in their bedroom.

Observations often complement the ideas you might already have about how a child has reacted to earlier life events that you will be aware of from a referral or from gathering historical information. Fahlberg (1991, p.238) comments on how 'direct observations provide either confirmation or denial of the suspected perceptions and/or underlying need'. It is important that observation is always seen in the broader context of the evidence of past and present relationships:

> Observational evidence may be revealing but what matters is not an interaction at a particular point in time, but the whole history of the relationship and what it has to tell us about the child's deep-rooted feelings about self and others in relationships, the attachment pattern of the child. (Schofield 1998)

We must never allow a child's age or stage of development to limit his capacity for communication. Observations are key in *all* assessments particularly when considering relationships, but for infants, toddlers and children who have significant cognitive impairments, observations are likely to be your key source of direct information. Howe *et al.* (1999, p.178) argue this is because

> so much of the information we need to make sense of the quality of relationships and caregiving environment can only be gained by observation of the family's physical environment, the interactions between family members and the impact of those interactions on the individual, parent or child.

It is not sufficient to accept self-reporting of the quality of relationships within families; you need to see it, hear it, smell it, feel it. Think about how to see both parents or caregivers. Can you observe parenting tasks at different times of the day? At breakfast time or when getting ready for school and at bedtime, you really see parenting. Also think about seeing parenting in different contexts, not only at home, but maybe at the park or at the supermarket, where there may be more variables or challenges.

Whilst there is undoubtedly an argument for 'intimate' engagement with children and families (Ferguson 2016), I feel there is also tremendous benefit *at times* to be gained by standing back. The key skill in observation is in establishing clarity around exactly what it is you are observing and an interpretation or understanding of what you see. To do this effectively it is essential to have some underpinning of normative child development, together with an awareness of the 'potential for discrimination and cultural bias where abstract norms are rigidly applied' (Lefevre 2008b, p.27). Some helpful ideas to have in your mind, based on your knowledge of typical child development include the following prompts:

- Does the child look and act his age?

- Does he explore his environment?

- Does he have to touch everything?

- Does he seem confident or tentative in his social approaches?

- Is he focused or easily distracted from a task, play or conversation? Is this typical of a child of his age?

- What's his general presentation? How would you sum him up?

- Does he test limits or is he compliant with requests?

- What does he say?

During periods of observation, it is also important to notice your own emotional responses to the environment, to the child and to the family and take this to supervision to maintain your focus on the child. Also vital is maintaining conscious awareness of judgements we may be led to make based on our own cultural norms. Shaw (in Dunhill *et al.* 2009, p.63) reminds us that:

> even within the family home, communication and engagement are doubly difficult when the family is from a different background to the childcare worker, either in terms of race or class. Norms which exist in one culture or group may not be reflected in another and it is difficult to differentiate where a difference is cultural, a reflection of genuine cause for concern or simply poor communication.

Periods of observation don't need to take hours. For example, if you time your visit well to a school, in 90 minutes you could observe arrival into school and separation from caregiver/parent, carpet time, a more structured lesson and then free play at break time. Hasler (in Hendry and Hasler 2017), writing about the work of Catchpoint with families who have experienced trauma, explains their assessments go across three settings. There will be a home visit to look at how the child responds to a stranger coming into the home and talking to his parents. The second will be a school observation to consider how the child manages in structured and unstructured contexts, with his peers and how he copes with transitions. This is a good opportunity to talk with his teachers too. The third is in a clinical setting where structured and unstructured activities are set up and the session is recorded to play back to the parent.

You need to *observe* behaviour (this will give you clues as to the feelings that impact the quality of the relationship) rather than *interpreting* behaviour to fit a particular narrative or hypothesis. Notice not just what is said or what is done, but how – the timing of approaches, the non-verbal communications (eye contact, proximity, facial expression) and the verbal encounters (consider language and tone of voice, as well as what is being said.) Does the parent offer consistent responses and does he demonstrate the capacity to tune in to the child's cues and therefore sensitively meet his attachment needs? How does the child overtly signal those needs? Is the caregiver both physically and emotionally available? Does the parent offer comfort and can the child accept caregiving? Is the child only addressed by his parent/caregiver when he is adjudged to have misbehaved? Is he invited to contribute to conversations or asked to be quiet? Does the caregiver seem aware that the child is a separate individual with needs of his own, or are the child's behaviours and communication always directly related back to what the parent needs? Are expectations appropriate for the child's age and developmental stage?

When you are recording your observations, also be mindful of the language you use. Nicholas (2016) reminds us:

> The words inappropriate and/or appropriate are judgement words. What one person considers inappropriate another may consider to be absolutely fine and therefore by writing 'the child was inappropriately dressed' or 'the child was using inappropriate language', that is your

view, but it means nothing. Beyond that as with all recording you really should spell out what the child and/or the adult was actually doing.

I would advise using an observation template saved in a landscape format to help to organise your thinking and be clear about what the purpose of the observation is. Record the child's name and age, the date, time of day, where and for how long the observation took place. Then have headings to help you focus the lens through which you're observing the child and family, for example (adapted from Leeds City Council's Practitioner Assessment Resource Pack):

- What was happening during the observation? What was the general activity? (e.g. breakfast time, bedtime, getting ready to leave for school)

- What did you notice about the environment?

- What did you notice about how the child was feeling? Did this change during the observation? What made you think he was feeling X at that time? How could you tell?

- What did you notice about how the parent/carer was feeling? Did this change during the observation? What made you think he was feeling X at that time? How could you tell?

- Did the child try to gain his parent/carer's attention? If so, how? What did you notice about his verbal and non-verbal communication? Was it age-appropriate?

- How did the parent/carer respond or react when the child made these overtures? Did he seem to accurately interpret the child's need or communication? What did you observe in terms of physical proximity, closeness or affection/nurture?

- Were there times when parent and child disagreed or when there was a rupture in the relationship? Was there repair following this? How did they both respond?

- Was anyone else in the house? How did they interact? Did this make a difference to the child's presentation or the family dynamic?

- Any other observations? How did you feel during the observation? Were there any surprises, challenges or learnings? Will anything need further assessment or exploration? Has the observation yielded information that may support or disconfirm an existing hypothesis?

Hasler (2017, pp.87–89) uses a more attachment specific lens for her observation table highlighting elements of attachment behaviour and then what is being observed (Table 6.1). Looking at behaviours with an attachment focus is different to doing an assessment of 'attachment relationships' or 'bonding'.

Table 6.1 Catchpoint assessment observations

Element of attachment behaviour	What is being observed
Response to strange people and places	Stranger visiting home or child visiting strange place – is the child: • Charming and engaging? • Avoidant or dismissive?
Exploration	How the child explores unusual objects – does the child: • Share exploration with parents? • Ask questions about the instruments? • Avoid exploring at all?
Reciprocity	Taking turns – is the child able to: • Take turns and wait for his turn? • Take part in a reciprocal conversation?
Emotional expression	Range of emotional expressions – does the child show: • Appropriate or inappropriate emotional expressions? • Flat emotional presentation?
Peer friendships	Different settings, structured and unstructured – how does the child: • Respond to working with peers in a classroom setting? • Respond to peers at play time?
Representation of family	The family are invited to draw a picture of what they do together – does the child: • Engage in discussion with parents about the picture? • Represent all or part of the family? • Use relationship terms?
Separation and reunion	Parent leaves the room without saying where he is going – does the child: • Enquire where the parent has gone? • Respond when the parent returns? • Show parent what he has been doing while separated?

cont.

Transition	Observing child moving between structured and unstructured activities – how does the child: • Respond to change of activity? • Move out to playground? • Respond to being asked to line up? • Come back into the classroom?
Chaos and order	How does the child organise himself: • Is he chaotic or over-ordered? • Does he create a feeling of chaos?
A sense of self	Inner working models – does the child: • Present as needing or not needing adults? • Show confidence or lack of confidence? • Accept or reject praise? • Celebrate achievement? • Have a sense of shared humour?
Control	Observations of the child's need to be in control – does the child: • Accept control from adults? • Listen to instructions? • Try to take control through subtle or overt means?
Hypervigilance	Observations of child's awareness of the immediate environment – does the child: • Appear to be watchful and aware? • Notice sounds outside the room? • Sit where he can see the rest of the room?
Dissociation	Indicators of dissociative behaviours – does the child show: • Repetitive behaviours such as rocking, fiddling, chewing? • Incessant chatting with no purpose? • Switching off? • Sudden changes of behaviour, voice or skills?

Source: Hasler (2017, pp.87–89), reproduced with permission

Non-directive or free play

When we are busy we tend to move towards more directive activities imagining this will yield the information we seek more quickly, but this is to minimise the potential of observing and facilitating (without interference or interpretation) non-directive play. I have already described what might be contained in a creative toolkit (Chapter 2), but also consider offering the child access to other toys like dolls, bricks or LEGO®, a doctor's kit, toy telephone or puppets.

Play is one way in which young children make sense of their world. They will play out positive as well as negative experiences. When we meet the child where he is, we are in a much better position to assess need and where necessary offer protection and advocacy. The younger the child is, the more quickly he forgets events; the capacity to recall past events, even very familiar or frequent ones, is very limited before the age of three. This is significant if we are trying to clarify specific episodes in a family story or where we believe abuse has occurred. Verbal recall can be difficult for little people. There is evidence that children will recall stressful events more vividly, especially if they were experienced as threatening or negative. However, this recall is likely to be related to how the child felt rather than in factual detail (Jones 2003).

In non-directive play contexts, follow the child, rather than taking the lead yourself, and this will inform your assessment as you learn about how the child functions, relates and communicates. Imaginative play usually begins early into the second year, as the child draws on his experiences. In the third year, you may see the development of imaginary friends and using objects to represent other things (e.g. sand to represent dinner). You may begin to hear commentaries on the play and the use of different voices. You might not understand the messages initially, but by offering a neutral commentary and reflecting back what you think you see, this helps the child understand you are attending to him. Conversations (both verbal and non-verbal) can then begin to emerge, together with a better understanding of what's happening in the child's world.

Never assume you know what it is that is being played out, but be alert to factors that may suggest re-enactment of an event the child has experienced or witnessed. If this is the case, you may notice a higher level of detail and language or understanding that is at odds with other interactions you have observed. You might hear words or phrases that sound more adult or unusual for a child of that age or stage. The same sequence of play may be repeated several times, which can be indicative of children trying to process or make sense of their experiences. Some children will become highly aroused (or stressed) during the play and may need nurture (a drink, snack, physical touch or a teddy) or to have a break (expect requests to go to the toilet, leave the room, check where the parent/caregiver is) (Tait and Wosu 2013).

This chapter offers structured activities that will support your gaining an understanding what a typical day in the life of a child and his family looks and feels like. However, don't forget to ask the child or young person the best way to learn about his world. A recent three-year nationwide study, Talking and Listening to Children, identified that it wasn't the application of a specific tool or direct work technique that was most important in terms of engaging children, but rather the subtleties of relationships that were unique for each child and family. (You can find out more about this project and access resources at www.talkingandlisteningtochildren.co.uk.)

A DAY IN THE LIFE

Materials

Paper and pens.

Process

This activity can be done with a school-aged child creatively or you can use the question prompts with parents/carers. You will want to consider both school days as well as weekends/school holidays when routines might differ. You can ask the child to map out the day pictorially, splitting the page into boxes to represent different parts of the day and ask him to show you what each time of day looks like.

Getting up	Going to school	The school day	After school	Evening	Bedtime

Figure 6.1 A Day in the Life table

Or you can draw a timeline and complete it together from getting up at 7am, for example, to going to bed at 9pm.

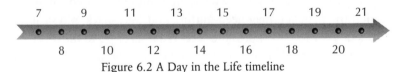

Figure 6.2 A Day in the Life timeline

Here are some prompts (adapted from Horwath 2007):

Morning

How does he get up in the morning?

What time does he wake, or is woken?

Is there a regular routine?

Does the child take responsibility for other siblings or for parents/carers?

Who makes sure everyone is up in time?

Does he have anything to eat?

Is there usually something to eat for breakfast in the house?

Does an adult supervise or make breakfast?

Does the child buy something on the way to school? If so what?

Does the child go to breakfast club at school? Is he fed at nursery or pre-school?

What about getting dressed and ready for the day?

Are clothes ready and clean? Is there a routine for this?

Does the child have to find his own clothes? Choose his own clothes?

Does he have his own clothing?

What about having a wash, brushing teeth and hair? Is this prompted or supervised by an adult?

Is there a hairbrush, soap, toothbrush and toothpaste available?

If the child bed-wets, is he encouraged to bathe/shower before school?

Getting to school

What happens if he is going to school?

How does he get to school?

Does an adult take him?

What is the journey to school? For example, a 30-minute walk including crossing a dual carriageway or five-minute walk across a playing field?

Does he take younger brothers and sisters? Does he walk with friends?

What happens at school?

How does he get along with teachers?

What does he do when he arrives in the playground? Does he have anyone to play with at break and lunch time?

What does he like to do at school? What doesn't he like?

What does he eat at lunchtime?

Is he in any clubs at school?

Does he get bullied?

After school
What happens after school?

Does he get collected from school? On time?

Does he stay for after school activities?

Does he see friends after school/play out?

What is the journey home from school like?

What happens when he gets home?

Is food available?

Does he take care of anyone when he gets home? Other brothers and sisters? Carers/parents/other adult relatives?

What happens if it's the weekend/holidays?

Would he be expected to look after siblings/parents/carers?

Does he have to do jobs in the house/run errands?

What happens about food?

Is he supervised by an adult? Does someone know where he is?

Evening/night time

Does he have a bedtime?

Who decides when he goes to bed?

Where does he sleep? What kind of bedding does he have?

Does he change his clothes before bed?

Does he have a wash and brush his teeth?

Does he get disturbed when he is trying to sleep? This could be because others in the house are making a noise or because he has nightmares, for example.

Is he left alone at night? Is he expected to look after other children when parents/caregivers go out or are otherwise unavailable?

When you have completed this activity (it can help to have a template saved in landscape for ease of use), reflect on what you have heard. Can you identify what is missing in the care of the child? How many dimensions of the child's needs are being met or are at risk? What appears to be the impact of this on the child's development, presentation or wellbeing? What are your thoughts about the likelihood that improvements can be made in the child's timeframe? Do any changes need to be made and how significant are they? How can you verify any information?

✓ Aims

– To gain a solid understanding of a child's or young person's daily routine; this will help you focus on the child's lived experience.

– To identify positives or strengths as well as highlighting areas of concern or risk in respect of neglect.

– To look at parenting capacity in relation to daily life, especially thinking about expectations of the child from a developmental perspective.

👍 Handy hints

Some children who lack confidence in their artistic abilities will sometimes benefit in exercises like this from your bringing along images you have googled – for example to represent times of the day, breakfast food, a school building, toiletries, a bath. They can then stick them on the image. You might also want to bring emojis or feelings faces, which again are easily made or downloaded, so the child can indicate non-verbally how he feels about certain tasks or times of the day. You can also use cue cards with adults and children from age eight with prompts based on key areas.

When working with young carers you will need to measure the extent of the caregiving tasks and the positive and negative outcomes associated with these additional responsibilities. Joseph, Becker and Becker (2009) have developed assessment tools for this, which include additional resources to inform both assessment of need and support for young people.

SIX-PART STORY MAKING

✂ Materials
Paper and felt pens or coloured pencils. You might want to prepare a six-part grid. Consider having the option of A4 or A3 paper.

✏ Process
This exercise was originally developed to identify coping strategies in individuals within the Arab and Israeli communities who were suffering from high levels of stress. The Six-Part Story method was introduced as an attempt to encourage creativity in assessment. Both Mooli Lahad, who was the originator of this method and Alida Gersie, another expert in this storytelling technique, use 'story making as a therapeutic technique for clients to project their own stories based on elements contained in fairy tales or myths' (Jennings et al. 1994, p.24).

In assessments, we can use this method to engage a child and gain some insight into his coping mechanisms and experience and understanding of the world. Invite the child to create a story using six stages, based on the basic components of traditional fairy tales. Lead him through the story step by step, by first dividing a large piece of paper into six sections; one for each stage of the story.

Hero and where s/he lives	Mission/task	Someone/ thing helpful
The obstacle	Overcoming the obstacle	Ending

Figure 6.3 Six-Part Story table

In the first box, encourage the child to draw the main character and where he/she lives. The character can be anyone, but do encourage the child to work within the realms of fiction or fantasy. In the second stage, the main character is given a task or mission to fulfil and the third stage is to create someone or something that assists the main character in the mission. The fourth part depicts an obstacle that impedes the character in completing the mission and the fifth picture shows how he overcomes it. In the sixth box, the child shows how the story ends, or indeed whether it reaches a conclusion at all.

This formula of hero/heroine, mission, helper, obstacle or monster, coping strategies or means of overcoming and an ending is one that gives the child a framework within which to explore his secret wishes (through the hero and the mission), the difficulties he faces in his life (through the obstacle/monster) and his way of coping or overcoming these difficulties by arriving at a satisfactory conclusion.

To complete this exercise in one session, allow about 40 minutes to draw the images, at the most, so as to leave time for storytelling. Some children may want to carry on the process over a number of sessions if time allows, developing quite elaborate pictures and complex stories. Others may prefer to expand each picture to talk about the feelings it evokes. Occasionally, children feel unable to do very much at all. This is not a major problem as often, once they have grasped the method, they find repeating the exercise more accessible. Some children will need a lot of guidance and encouragement, whilst others like to work almost unaided. It's always important to follow the child's lead and only offer assistance or scaffolding if it is required or requested.

Once the Six-Part Story is completed, allow the child/young person time to tell you the story using their pictures and six stages as prompts. Allow him to do this as uninterrupted as you can, as this helps to ensure you don't impose your own understandings or interpretations of the story. To summarise the steps:

1. Character/hero and where s/he lives

2. Mission/task

3. Someone or something that helps

4. The obstacle or monster they will meet

5. How the character copes with the obstacle

6. The ending/what happens next

✓ Aims

– To gain insight into the child's experience of the world.

– To explore the child's coping strategies.

– To allow exploration through metaphor which allows for a 'one step removed' sense of safety.

👍 Handy hints

Using stories can support a child or young person to communicate in a way that may be experienced as more tolerable or less threatening than more direct and conventional talking methods.

It can help provide safety to communicate underlying feelings and thoughts, especially if he is in a situation where he is inhibited from effectively communicating feelings. For example, it may be easier to symbolically express a fear of dragons or a giant child-eating spider, than to talk about being frightened at home of your step-parent. This technique can help start a dialogue about fear that may not have otherwise occurred.

There are ways of expanding on the story if time permits. Opportunities can be created for the child to project feelings from or about the story onto objects or toys. The child/young person could stage a picture from the story using a selection of miniatures from your toolkit (see also Sculpting exercise in Chapter 5). This can help to further explore any aspect you or the child want to look at in more depth. This exploration may allow a fairly simple statement of feelings but could also enable more complex connections with the child's life to be made and explored. It allows the child to set the pace in a non-threatening way using his own level of communication and helps greatly in the process of relationship building.

The story can also be acted out with the child/young person in the role of the hero/heroine. This process can expand on the story as new elements are brought into play.

With thanks to Lesley Naylor for her work on this exercise.

WELCOME MAT

Materials
Rectangular paper or lining paper and pens/crayon.

Process
Suggest the child creates a Welcome Mat (like the ones usually placed before a front door in the home). He can include images or words to represent himself and his past, current or future home. You might decide to offer the choice or guide the child as to which home to depict, depending on what information would most inform your assessment. If you were working on a larger sheet of paper or on lining paper, you could split it into three and ask the child to draw past, present and future homes alongside

each other for comparison. The practitioner can then explore the meaning of the message or the design on the mat with the child. For example, does the mat look welcoming, warm and inviting or does it seem to represent chaos and fear? Would you want to come into this house? Who lives in the house?

✓ Aims

- To gain understanding of the child's lived experience – what represents *home* and what does this mean for his everyday life?

- To understand more about the physical and emotional environment in which the child lives.

- To help the child express feelings about different places he has lived.

- To support exploration of the child's hopes, dreams and expectations for the future. If a drawing of a future home is dramatically altered from his current home, you will potentially see indicators of what might need to change.

👍 Handy hints

This activity could also be used with adult family members to gain perspective on his past and current living situation. You might also ask parents/carers to make a Welcome Mat to represent their child's future home, which could reveal insight either into what might need to change to improve the family's situation or what he might want to be different in the future.

Where families have experienced multiple moves or where the safety of the home may vary depending on who is living there, you could invite making multiple Welcome Mats to allow you to isolate contextual changes in the home environment and the impact this may have had on lived experiences.

MY HOUSE OR MY CASTLE

✂ Materials

A doll's house with furniture and dolls or a castle with soldiers. If this isn't possible then you can use templates of house or castle outlines, preferably enlarged to A3 size with felt-tip pens.

✎ Process

This is an adaptation of an exercise developed by the NSPCC (1997). Depending on the child's interests and personality, use either a house or a castle analogy. Describe the house/castle, directing him to the front door or drawbridge on which you have written: PLEASE KNOCK AND WAIT. Explore with the child who might live there. Is it his home? If not, who might we find if we go inside? Where are the people in the house and what are they doing? How does he feel about the people or the rooms he describes?

You can expand this to think about which areas of the home are private and who might be allowed inside. Is there anywhere in the home that doesn't feel safe or comfortable? This is also potentially a helpful approach to use with children living in a residential setting – either in a mainstream children's home or with children with additional needs who may access short breaks. It can help you to explore routines in the home and who does what. Where does the child spend most of his time and with whom, doing what?

✓ Aims

– To explore the child's everyday experience.

– To explore family relationships in the context of safety and expression of emotion.

– To assess understanding of personal space and privacy.

– To connect feelings with people or places in the child's life.

👍 Handy hints

If there is a likelihood the child has been abused in the family home or placement, you will need to approach this exercise with caution. If you are using the activity as part of an investigative process, be mindful of avoiding leading questions that could compromise any criminal investigation that may follow.

If using templates, you could expand this exercise to support further exploration of feelings towards other family members, by asking the child to draw them in the house doing what they would do on a typical day. You could suggest adding thought or speech bubbles to help you understand what people are thinking or feeling. You may need to prompt with questions that will increase understanding. For example: 'I wonder who that is? What is she thinking right now?' Try to explore different areas of family life and times of the day, as well as when people might feel happy, sad, angry, etc. You could have some feelings faces to use to help the child attach a feeling to a room or a person.

The castle option has the advantage of being able to bring a dungeon into the scenario, into which the child can choose to place people who may have caused him harm. He could have soldiers to protect the castle walls from unsafe people or a moat filled with piranhas or crocodiles to keep unsafe people out. Ask the child when he would choose to raise the drawbridge and to whom he would deny entry? Might the excluded people be able to do anything now or in the future that would make them safe enough to allow entry into the castle or out of the dungeon?

MY THREE HOUSES

✂ Materials

Pens and paper or three pre-prepared house templates.

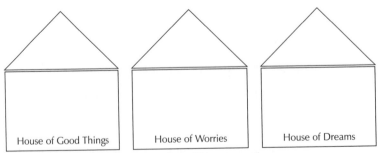

Figure 6.4 My Three Houses templates

Process

This tool was originally created by Nicki Weld and Maggie Greening in New Zealand (Turnell and Edwards 1999). Taking three diagrams of houses in a row, the practitioner explores the three key assessment questions of the Signs of Safety framework (Bunn 2013):

- What are we worried about?

- What's working well?

- What needs to happen/how would things look if they were as wanted?

Begin either by offering three blank houses to the child or asking him to draw three houses. Remember that it is okay to adapt the houses to reflect specific cultural contexts and diversity. I would usually begin with the 'House of Good Things'. Ask the child what the best things are about living in the house, directly enquiring about positive things that the child enjoys doing there and with whom?

Next, progress to the 'House of Worries' to establish if there are things that worry the child in the house or things or people that he doesn't like. Finally, the 'House of Dreams' allows you to consider thoughts and beliefs the child has about how the house would be if it was just as he desired. You can help him to build up a description that explains who would be living there, and what would happen day to day in this house.

When you've finished think about whether it would be appropriate to ask the child if he would be happy to show parents/relatives/carers.

Aims

- To explore the child's everyday experience.

- To facilitate exploration of strengths and resilience, worries, hopes and dreams.

- To explore family relationships.

 **Handy hints**

The My Three Houses app brings this tool into the digital realm with video, interactive animation and a drawing pad for children. It also includes a video explanation for parents and extensive guidance for workers. Most importantly the app makes it easier for workers who have limited time to do the most important and often hardest part of their job – getting vulnerable children to speak. It can be downloaded for free, and further information is available at www.mythreehouses.com.

DOLL'S HOUSE PLAY

Materials

A doll's house with furniture and dolls representing people of different ages. This is easier if you are working from a playroom with a doll's house *in situ*, but you can source portable fold-and-go doll's houses (e.g. by Playmobil) that are much easier to transport in your boot.

Alternatively, if you want to try to offer the child a house that more closely resembles his own, you could try making one with him, but this will require more time. You can of course be talking about the child's own home while you're making. You'll need boxes (e.g. cereal), sturdy tape, glue, card, felt tips, furniture and doll figures. The figures can be homemade too, using pipe cleaners, pegs or wooden spoons or modelling materials like Plasticine.

Process

This is a great opportunity to simply observe some free play with children, informing your assessment in terms of who is important in the child's world, who lives at home and who visits the home from the community. Consider the nature of the play and how the child uses the objects. What is the quality of the interactions? Is the child slow and measured in his actions? Is he hypervigilant and wary of your responses? Is he chaotic or hyperactive?

It is also a chance to observe many other aspects of the child's global development, especially if you are working together on building his house from scratch. Notice his verbal and non-verbal communication skills, his fine motor skills – can he use scissors, cut tape, colour in? How well does he stay on-task, ask for or accept help if he needs it? How does he manage if something goes wrong in the construction or in the play? Can he tolerate disappointment or distraction? Can he use his imagination? Can he role-play? Can he follow your instructions?

In free play, try not to be too intrusive or ask closed questions that might shut down communication. Similarly, don't assume you know whom the dolls represent – be curious about this or make statements that reflect what you are seeing without making interpretations. This evidences to the child that you are interested and paying attention. Follow the play, making observations and commenting and even naming feelings in a curious, wondering way.

✓ Aims

– To gain understanding of the child's lived experience – what represents *home* and what does this mean for his everyday life?

– To understand more about the physical and emotional environment in which the child lives.

– To observe free play.

– To explore both who lives in and visits the home.

☝ Handy hints

It can be helpful, especially if you are using a doll's house in a room that will be used by other workers and children, to photograph stages of the play. It is unlikely to look the same if you come back to the room another day (indeed in our playroom we ask that the doll's house is cleared at the end of the session) and that way you can reflect on the images next time you meet, if that would seem helpful. You will also have an aide memoire when writing up the session notes later as this is not a time for note writing with the child present.

Tait and Wosu (2013) expand further on the practicalities of constructing your own model house and offer a case example if you need further guidance.

CHAPTER 7

TALKING ABOUT A SPECIFIC EVENT

In assessments, there is often a need to establish a set of facts surrounding an event or to understand how an individual has experienced an incident, a relationship or an interaction. There are lots of complications and potential pitfalls when we set out to find 'the truth'; not least because key players will have different perceptions of events or actions, because evidence can be limited to one person's word against another, and because it is rare for professional intervention in family life to be related to a single issue. In cases of domestic abuse, for example, there will commonly also be concerns around parental mental health, substance abuse and emotional harm to the child (Cafcass and Women's Aid 2017).

The additional barriers faced by traumatised people in talking about distressing experiences or recounting them coherently have also already been explored in earlier chapters. Yet still we need to help vulnerable children and families tell their stories with sensitivity, if we are to undertake a robust, trauma-informed and child-focused assessment. Understanding just how vulnerable the process of storytelling can be will make you a better support when you are helping others tell their stories. Sometimes unexpected emotions and memories emerge when you both tell and hear a story; in assessments we will be alongside people as they make an important transition, sometimes for the first time, where experiences become separate from the person, as they are witnessed by another.

In our efforts to establish a coherent narrative, we must not underestimate the impact of physical and emotional trauma on memory systems in the brain. At times memory loss may be a temporary state to help an individual cope with the trauma, but with complex trauma, *explicit memory* ('the conscious intentional recollection of factual information, previous experiences and concepts': Ullman 2004) can be also impaired, which means that it can be difficult for survivors to recall specific facts or events. This is important in assessment terms, as we utilise explicit memory throughout the day for diverse tasks; for example, remembering the time of an assessment session or recalling an event from our early childhood. However, memory and recall are complex processes, as individual as trauma victims themselves. Trauma can impact memory of the traumatic event, memories of preceding or subsequent events or even thoughts in general terms. There is evidence that long-term memory is most commonly affected by psychological trauma (Squire 1987).

Stress can also impact an individual's capacity to encode memory and to retrieve information. If we assume that an assessment session may be experienced as a stressful event, then we should expect that when we ask individuals to recall details of a traumatic event this might be problematic. His body will secrete stress hormones into the bloodstream and frequently this will impair memory. When the body is in a state of chronic stress over a long period of time, the fight-or-flight response is activated; this too will negatively affect memory and learning. The pre-frontal cortex – the part of the brain responsible for executive or higher-order functions – is also impaired by stress and in some extreme cases will go offline, shut down by a stream of stress hormones. Under these circumstances, it is more difficult to control what we pay attention to, to make sense of what we are experiencing and recall our experience coherently.

When terror or alarm kicks in, the brain's fear circuitry (specifically the amygdala) takes over. This alters the functioning of another key area of the brain called the hippocampus, which means that the capacity to encode experiences into short-term memory and then subsequently store them as long-term memory is limited. Fear also impacts the capacity of the hippocampus to store contextual information and to encode time-sequenced information. This is significant when you are asking an individual to recount a traumatic event such as a sexual assault or incident of domestic abuse. The victim may be able to remember in high levels of detail what was happening just before and after they were attacked, but is likely to have very fragmented and incomplete memories of the trauma itself (Hopper and Lisak 2014).

In the aftermath of a traumatic event, the brain will be unable to recall many details that might be significant to the assessment, and that were and may still be irrelevant to immediate survival.

The developmental capacity to tell our story also takes some time to come online. Younger children will be able to tell stories about isolated events, but it isn't until late adolescence and early adulthood that our capacity for story construction is really consolidated under normal developmental conditions. By then, individuals have typically developed the cognitive tools needed to create a coherent life story. A German study that analysed the life stories of 8-, 12-, 16- and 20-year-olds identified that *causal coherence* (the ability to describe how one event led to another) and *thematic coherence* (the ability to identify overarching values and motifs that recur throughout the story) increased with age (Beck 2015). *Narrative coherence* is the way in which we organise a narrative into a sequence that is meaningful to the self and the listener. All parts of the story must fit together so the entire sequence relates in a meaningful way. Between four and six years of age, typically developing children can begin to recount coherent narratives and personal reports as well as creating their own detailed stories (Cavalcante and Mandra 2010). This is important to hold in mind when you are working with children and young people to understand an event in their lives.

Remember also that the stories we tell about our lives are influenced by more than just ourselves. The way we tell the story to others shapes how we remember events. The perception or response of others to that story is also highly significant. Inevitably in an assessment context, individuals may tailor the story to the audience and context. There are clearly consequences to telling and to not telling. If people have not spoken before about historic events that you are then asking about in the assessment, the memory of the event may have become quite fixed. If they have told the story before and had negative or unhelpful feedback, this will also influence the re-telling. For some, expressing thoughts and feelings either orally or in writing about difficult or traumatic events seems to help wellbeing, but if the story doesn't fit a standard or typical narrative, then there is an added risk of feeling stigmatised.

In this chapter you will find structured exercises that will help provide a framework for children and adults to explore events or incidents in family life, for example an assault, running away or self-harm. They will support you in safely enabling the telling of these stories and the exploration of associated feelings and perceptions. It is imperative you do all you can to ensure that these sessions, and indeed your practice, is trauma-informed at all times.

WHAT'S THE WEATHER LIKE? OR WEATHER REPORT

✂ Materials

Pen and paper or pre-prepared weather state flash cards, preferably laminated so you can re-use them.

🖉 Process

Supporting a child or young person to talk about his perception of a situation or an event can sometimes be difficult. There can be many reasons for this. The child may have muddled up or confused feelings. He might be embarrassed to talk about how things feel for him. He might be worried about the consequences of telling. He may not have with words or emotional literacy skills to name or recognise feelings. He may have a disability or communication difficulties that limit his capacity to explore lived experiences.

However, in undertaking an assessment with a child or young person, it is crucial to try and obtain his thoughts and feelings about the situation he is living in. This is a simple exercise that can be used at various stages in an assessment process. Begin by introducing the idea of different weather states – picture flashcards can help show what you mean. For example:

Warm and sunny

Cold and icy

Stormy

Rainy

Cloudy with sunny intervals

Cloudy or overcast

Figure 7.1 Weather symbols

You need to spend some time first exploring how each weather state feels and any associated thoughts and feelings the child might be able to name. For example, *warm and sunny* may elicit memories of playing at the park, holidays or positive thoughts and feelings of joy. *Cold and icy* might suggest loneliness or isolation. Don't skip on this preparation; if you do, it may mean the child will find it more difficult to move on to the next stage of the exercise.

Depending upon the focus of your session, use the cards to support the child to attribute a weather state to a context (e.g. school or home), to a relationship or to a specific event (e.g. the death of a sibling or exclusion from school). You can do this verbally, draw an image or even write a weather report, similar to what you might hear read out on the news. For example:

> *Today the weather conditions were mixed. It was a fine, dry start to the day at school, but soon became grey and overcast in Maths after a thunderstorm in the corridor with some Year 8 boys. My learning mentor came to try to help clear the fog but it settled until lunchtime. The sun came out in the afternoon during PE and I hope it will be sunny throughout the evening. That's it for today – there will be a further update in the morning.*

✓ Aims

– To explore the child's lived experience.

– To explore thoughts and feelings about a specific event, context or relationship.

– To assist exploration of difficult themes or feelings through metaphor, increasing a sense of safety in the individual.

For the extension exercise in 'Handy hints':

– To make connections between felt sensations in the body with emotions and externalise these.

– To notice where in the body these senses are held and create a dialogue between body and mind.

👍 Handy hints

You don't have to use all the weather states and certainly for a younger child you may just choose a few to avoid overwhelming him.

An adaptation of this idea is the Weather Report. Ask the child to sit up straight in a chair with both feet on the floor and to relax the neck and shoulders as much as possible. If it feels safe to do so, he should close his eyes and breathe calmly and slowly. Explain how hard it can be to express how our body is feeling, though it feels so many different things. Ask how he feels in the here and now. Does his body feel relaxed? How fast or slow is his heartbeat? Ask him to pay attention to his chest and stomach area next. How is it feeling? Can he go inside and sense his internal weather?

When he feels fine his internal weather might be sunny and bright with not a cloud in the sky. When he is feeling angry he could feel a storm is brewing or there could be a thunderstorm inside. If he is feeling sad or lonely, he might say it's raining inside. Ask how he is feeling inside right now. Is there a combination of different kinds of weather to report? Is it cloudy with a hint of sunshine peeking through? Is it brisk and breezy? Is there a chance the internal weather might change, just as the weather outside often does? For example, the sunshine might be hidden by clouds or a rainy day might be lit by a rainbow when the sun comes out.

Then imagine what the weather might look like – it might be a colour, a view or an image. Move on to depict an image of the weather inside the body on paper – sometimes young people can find it liberating to use their non-dominant hand to draw with, especially if they're unsure about their drawing abilities.

I find this exercise is best used with older children. When the young person has finished creating the image, check in with how he is feeling right at that moment. Is it different to the picture he has created? If it does seem different it is fine to add to or change the image. This reinforces the idea that feelings can shift and change in moments of time.

SECRETS AND SECRET ENABLERS

✂ Materials

Cards with a variety of different secrets – some good/safe/comfortable secrets and some bad/unsafe/uncomfortable secrets – and felt-tip pens.

🖉 Process

Explain to the child that whilst it can sometimes be good fun to keep a secret, it always depends on the kind of secret. There are two different kinds of secrets. Good secrets are usually only kept for a short while and when shared will usually make someone else feel good. Examples of good secrets could be a surprise party for a family member or a child winning a school prize.

A bad secret may mean someone feels unsafe, may need to be kept for ever, may not be shared with anyone or may come accompanied by a threat. If only two people know the secret, it is more likely to be a bad secret. A bad secret might give you an early-warning sign in your body and you should always tell someone on your safety network (see 'Identifying Personal Networks' in Chapter 3).

You might need to explain early-warning signs if the child is unaware. Explain that when someone is in a potentially dangerous situation, the body gets ready for action; we all experience real, physical feelings in different parts of our bodies that give us a clue this is happening and that we might not be safe. These early-warning signs tell us we may be at risk of harm, and we need to listen to our bodies so we can make choices to keep us safe. It may be a signal to ask for help if we can't sort the problem out on our own. These signs might include: sweating palms; blushing; shaking; breathing heavily; running away; heart rate increasing; stammering; throat tightening; headache; biting lips; butterflies in the tummy; or clenching fists.

Schonveld and Myko (1999) suggest some questions to help children when they're not sure about a secret and can't decide whether to tell a network person about it. I have summarised them here.

Questions to ask to decide whether a secret is 'good' or 'bad'

Does this secret give me an early-warning sign?

Does it mean I will have to do something I don't usually do?

Is the person sharing the secret someone I trust? Is s/he in my network?

What might stop me telling this secret?

Who am I supposed to be keeping this secret from?

Questions to ask about secret places

If I go to this place, can I get home or leave when I choose?

Can I get help when I am there and from whom?

Does anyone in my family or in my network know where I am?

Questions to ask about being alone with adults

Do I trust this person? If so, why?

Have I been on my own with this person before?

Do I feel safe with him/her/them?

Do my parents or carers know I'm with him/her/them? Would they approve?

There are different ways to explore this further. You might prepare a list of secrets on cards and ask the child to choose whether to put them in the 'safe secret' pile or the 'unsafe secret' pile. You could prepare the same statements on a worksheet and ask the child to colour the good secrets green and the bad secrets red.

Here are some examples of secrets to give some ideas, but do ensure the list of secrets you devise is relevant to the child you're working with and assessment context. If you have hypotheses about the child's experiences make sure these are reflected in the statements.

- Someone touched your private parts/vagina/penis/breasts/bottom.

- You made a gift to give your parent/carer for Christmas at school.

- The present you chose for your best friend's birthday gift.

- A child in your school is calling you unkind names when no one else is around.

- You saw somebody steal something from your local shop.

- Someone is regularly taking your school lunch money from you.

- The place where your family hides the spare key for emergencies.

- Where you keep your treasures.

- Your friend is being hit by his dad.

- Where you hide your pocket money for safe keeping.

- One parent has hit the other.

- You drank some alcohol at a party.

✓ Aims

- To support the child's understanding of the difference between good/safe/comfortable secrets and bad/unsafe/uncomfortable secrets.

- To teach the child he should never keep secrets about touching or experiencing early-warning signs and should always tell a network person if someone asks him to keep a 'bad secret'.

- To teach the child about secret enablers – strategies perpetrators use to get children to keep an unsafe secret. (See 'Handy hints' for more on this.)

👍 Handy hints

This is a game you might play in an assessment where you are concerned that a child has in some way been silenced – and cannot therefore talk about what has been happening in his life. It is also helpful where you hypothesise that the child is unaware that what he is experiencing is harmful. As you play this game, you will need to explore age-appropriate examples and ways in which children can be manipulated to keep secrets. Think about the following techniques that children have shared:

- *Threats* – warnings about what will happen if the child tells the secret; often that he or someone/something precious to him will be hurt or killed.

- *Tricks* – the abuse is made into a game or is connected in some sense with love or fun. For example, 'I do this to you because I love you' or 'Let's play the tickling game.'

- *Lies* – that no one will believe the child if he tells.

- *Guilt* – that it is the child's fault for 'leading the adult on' or that the child will be responsible for the adult going to prison or getting into trouble if he tells.

- *Bribes* – treats, gifts or special treatment if he cooperates and promises not to tell.

- *Shame* – that if the child tells, everyone will think he is 'bad' or naughty.

Remember that children may hold beliefs and fantasies about abusive situations that might seem utterly illogical to us as adults; yet when we consider children's responses in the context of their developmental age and stage, they can make much more sense. Younger children will naturally hold an egocentric view of the world and view themselves as responsible for everything that happens, even abuse. Older children while less egocentric in their thinking will also be quick at times to generate and justify the reasons why they must be to blame in some way.

HOT CROSS BUN

✂ Materials
Pen and paper or a Hot Cross Bun worksheet (these can easily be downloaded for free).

✐ Process
This is a really useful technique from cognitive behavioural therapy (CBT) (Padesky and Mooney, 1990), which is an approach underpinned by two main principles:

1. Our thoughts impact the way we feel and behave.

2. The way we interpret or understand a situation is impacted by the beliefs we have about ourselves, others and the world around us.

It can be used with people of any age to support them to tell you about a specific incident or event they have experienced. It may be helpful if you are investigating a particular concern, for example a domestic violence incident or act of physical harm against a child, as it can help both with information about *what* happened as well as exploring thoughts and feelings and the *how* and *why*.

A cross-sectional CBT formulation is also sometimes called the Hot Cross Bun and can be used to take a snapshot if all key aspects of the model during a single event. It can help individuals understand and explore how thoughts, feelings, bodily sensations and behaviours interact with each other. You can also take into account early or past experiences. Working in this way can help people make sense of issues that can otherwise feel overwhelming, by breaking them down into smaller component parts and then considering how different aspects influence or perpetuate the problem.

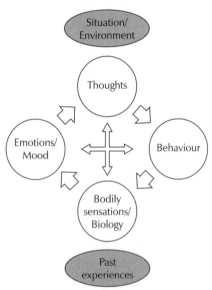

Figure 7.2 Hot Cross Bun

Padesky and Mooney (1990) explain how useful it can be to show people a written summary of the discussion. You can use the model to help people understand a particular problem (e.g. anxiety). Explain that we all live in a particular situation or environment (family, culture, weather) and are affected by what's happening in the here and now but also by what may have happened in our environment before. We all also have four aspects to ourselves, which are all interrelated and sit within our environment. Changes in just one of these domains (behaviour, emotions, physiology or thoughts) can impact on the others – positively or negatively.

Alternatively, you could simplify the task and ask the person to draw or write about the event in the first box, address thoughts about it in the second and feelings in the third.

What is happening?	What are you thinking?	What are you feeling?

Figure 7.3 Thoughts, feelings, behaviour

You may need to help with identifying feelings – this is where a little box of feelings cards or emojis can again come in very handy.

✓ Aims

- To support the child, young person or caregiver to tell you about a particular incident or event.

- To establish both the facts of the event as well as the thoughts and feelings attached to it.

👍 Handy hints

It can be hard sometimes for children and some adults to separate out thoughts from feelings. It might be helpful to give a brief, safe example to show what you intend for them to do in this exercise.

I was driving to a meeting but had set off later than planned. I was thinking I would be in trouble if I arrived at the meeting late. I was feeling anxious about what might be said about my late arrival and my heart had started to beat faster. I was aware of a tightness in my chest. I was afraid I might be stopped by the police for speeding.

TELLING MY STORY

Materials

Pen and pre-prepared script.

Process

Many years ago, when I was co-facilitating a therapy group for children aged 8–12 who had been sexually abused; we developed a tool to support sharing of their stories with the facilitators and other children in the group.[1] I have since used adaptations of this 'script' in many different settings to support children and young people to tell their stories without always having to speak the words. Here is a sample script you could use if someone has experienced sexual abuse, but please hold in mind that this must be adapted to fit individual circumstances, age and stage of development.

Be absolutely clear with the person that it is not necessary to answer every question and that some questions might have more than one answer. As it is set out in a multiple-choice style, it is possible to put a tick against as many of the answers as is appropriate. This helps recognise that people can hold seemingly contradictory stories, thoughts or feelings about people or events, and it normalises this ambivalence.

Some will choose to complete the script in silence and not speak at all of the event or of their thoughts and feelings about it. Others will use the script as a springboard from which to talk, in which case you can expand on the questions and your understanding of the experience to inform your assessment further.

---

1   It hopefully goes without saying that all the children were given the choice of whether to share their story or not.

TELLING MY STORY

REMEMBER: You can say/write as MUCH or as LITTLE as you want.

1. **Today I FEEL** . . . . **about telling my story.**

2. **The WORST thing that can happen while telling my story is:**

☐ you may not believe me

☐ I will be embarrassed

☐ I won't remember telling it

☐ I might feel really angry or upset

☐ I will have to remember what happened

☐ you could laugh

☐ you might not listen to me

☐ you may not understand

☐ or something else like . . . .

3. **I NEED you to:**

☐ listen when I am talking

☐ be kind to me

☐ be patient and not rush me

☐ let me have whatever feelings I want to have and show

☐ tell me what you think and feel about what I said

☐ let me have another safe adult I trust with me (parent/carer, teacher, neighbour)

4. **The PERSON or PEOPLE who hurt me was/were:**

☐ my mother

☐ my father

☐ my step-parent

☐ my mother's partner

☐ my brother or sister

☐ a neighbour

☐ a stranger

☐ my uncle/aunt

☐ my grandad/grandma

☐ a family friend

☐ and/or another person like . . . .

5. This HAPPENED to me:

☐ one or two times

☐ four or five times

☐ many times

☐ more times that I can count

6. The sexual abuse FELT:

☐ good sometimes

☐ horrible

☐ scary

☐ embarrassing

☐ painful

☐ weird/confusing

☐ I can't remember

☐ or something else like . . . .

7. AFTER it happened, I thought:

☐ I had done something wrong

☐ this happened to all boys and girls

☐ if I told someone then something terrible would happen to me

☐ there might be something wrong with my body

☐ I was special and loved

☐ people could tell I was abused by just looking at me

☐ that I should have stopped it but didn't know how

☐ no one would believe me if I told what had happened

8. I was given treats to keep quiet so he/she could carry on hurting me:

☐ cigarettes

☐ alcohol

☐ sweets

☐ being allowed to stay up late

☐ money

☐ or something else like . . . .

9. The person who sexually abused me TOLD ME:

☐ they would hurt me or someone special to me if I told someone

☐ nobody would believe me if I told

☐ never to tell

☐ that I was special and they loved me

☐ nothing

☐ that I was a disgusting person

☐ that they were doing nothing wrong

☐ it was my fault

☐ or other things like . . . .

10. After I told about the sexual abuse (or it was found out) I FELT:

. . . .

. . . .

11. The person who sexually abused me:

☐ went to prison

☐ had to leave my house

☐ is still living in my house

☐ got away with it

12. The worst thing about the abuse was:

. . . .

. . . .

. . . .

13. When I think of the person/people now I FEEL:

☐ disgusted

☐ sorry for them

☐ confused

☐ I miss them

☐ I want to see them again

☐ I wish they were dead

☐ afraid

14. The people who helped me or could help me were/are:

☐ family

☐ teachers/learning mentor

☐ youth worker

☐ police

☐ friends

☐ social workers

☐ pets

☐ someone else like . . . .

15. In the FUTURE I would like to be able to:

☐ tell my parents/carers how I feel

☐ walk tall and proud and not feel ashamed

☐ not feel afraid any more

☐ be able to make some more friends

☐ to stop having bad dreams

☐ or something else like . . . .

16. My three wishes for the future would be:

1 . . . .

. . . .

2 . . . .

. . . .

3 . . . .

. . . .

✓ Aims

– To support individuals to share information about a specific event that may have been experienced as traumatic.

– To allow individuals to share their stories without having to talk.

– To gain information you need about a specific event for assessment purposes – this could be historical information or in relation to a recent event.

☝ Handy hints

Pay careful consideration to the age and stage of the person you are working with as you design/amend your script. A similar version to this was originally used with primary-aged children, and we used lots of images to bring the script to life. If you were using this with an adolescent or an adult, this might be less appropriate and you might also need to adapt the language.

With thanks to Jan Hext for her work on this exercise.

BAG OF FEELINGS

✂ Materials

Paper, pens, template of a bag outline (optional).

✎ Process

This is a tool originally developed by clinical psychologists to assess children's feelings (Binney and Wright 1997). You can use this exercise to explore feelings about a specific incident, person or situation ongoing in the child's or family's life. What is generated is child-led, so you will gain a unique insight into the child's experiences. As an exercise, 'even with more communicative children, it can reveal information of greater depth than a more direct conversation about their problems or worries might' (Binney and Wright 1997, p.450) .

You should draw a bag (or have a template prepared) and say to the child: 'If this was a bag of all the feelings inside you, I wonder what would be inside there?'

Figure 7.4 Bag of Feelings

You might need to offer prompts, for example saying, 'You looked really nervous when you came in, I wonder how much of the bag would be filled with nervous feelings? Is that how you feel a lot of the time or just today?' Encourage the child to choose a colour to represent the feeling and draw it in the bag. Either you or the child should make a note of which colour represents which feeling. You can then either try to elaborate on each feeling state one by one, or fill the whole bag and then go back to explore each feeling separately. Whatever method you choose, try to elicit as much information as possible about that emotion.

When do you feel most nervous?

What happens when you feel nervous?

Where do you feel it in your body?

Can anyone help you when you feel this way?

Resist too much prompting or pressure as you risk yielding false results, especially with a child who is eager to please. However, you might offer prompts such as:

I see there are a lot of tricky feelings in your bag. Is there any room for good ones too?

What sort of feelings do you have when Mum asks you stay at home to look after the baby?

What about feelings to do with daddy/school/drugs?

✓ Aims

- To build rapport with the child or young person and validate his feelings and experiences.

- To elicit the child's feelings about people, events or life circumstances, which can then be linked with thoughts, beliefs and relationships. This is made easier by not having to use words.

- To gain a sense of the child's internal and external realities.

- To assess emotional literacy and the child's ability to articulate his emotional world.

- To aid understanding of the feelings and internal representations that the child has of himself and others.

Handy hints

This exercise was designed to be used in a 1:1 context, as the presence of a carer or sibling might inhibit the quality or truth of the information the child shares with you.

Some children feel more comfortable choosing a colour to represent a feeling without naming it. Binney and Wright (1997) feel this is acceptable and have found that blacks, purples and browns are more likely to represent negative affect, whereas blues, greens and yellows are more commonly associated with positive affect. It is important however not to make assumptions or interpret the colours too quickly. Follow up questions and your curiosity will usually reveal more about the quality of the child's emotion.

You could repeat this exercise at different phases of the assessment process. For example, as plans are put in place to address needs or risks, so the bag's contents may change. As well as using it to ascertain current states of mind it can also be used to think about how the child may have felt before (e.g. before grandma died or when in a previous foster placement) or may feel in the future (e.g. when his parent has stopped using heroin or when a new baby is born into the family).

Be mindful of how this session ends, especially if the bag is filled with very difficult feelings. You don't want the child to leave you feeling saturated by despair or rage. Think about a soft landing at the end of your time together, whether that's reading a story together, having a regulating snack or drink or doing a quick positive exercise to finish. Binney and Wright suggest putting three wishes into the bag. The wishes can also give you important information about what is realistic to hope for, whether the child can look more positively to the future or whether he has a sense of agency and self-efficacy.

BEHAVIOUR CHAIN ANALYSIS

- **Materials**
  Paper and pens.

- **Process**
  This is an exercise commonly used in dialectical behaviour therapy (DBT). It is a way of breaking down an event or a behaviour in very specific terms: a behavioural analysis (Davies 2017). In the first step, the specific problem behaviour is defined and you do a chain analysis together looking at the sequence of events and attempting to link one to another. As you do this you will generate hypotheses about what factors might be controlling or influencing the behaviour. You can then follow this with a solutions analysis where you consider alternative ways of dealing with the situation. Finally, you agree on a solution, thinking about what difficulties might be encountered and then working out strategies for dealing with them. Figure 7.5 adapted from www. dbtselfhelp.com/html/behavior_chain_analysis.html will help you work through a chain.

1. Describe the specific problem behaviour

   Describe the intensity of the behaviour – what else was important about it?

   What were you doing, thinking, feeling, imagining at the time?

   Describe what happened in enough detail that an actor could play the role perfectly

2. Describe the exact precipitating event

   What was going on when the event started?

   What were you doing, thinking, feeling, imagining at the time?

   Why did it happen that day and not the day before?

3. Describe in general terms the vulnerability factors that happened before the precipitating event

   Physical illness, disturbed sleep, injury?

   Drug or alcohol use?

   Stressful events in the environment? Previous behaviours of your own you find stressful?

   Intense emotions such as sadness, fear, loneliness or anger?

4. What chain of events led up to the problem behaviour? Links can be thoughts, emotions, sensations or behaviours

   How long is the chain? What are the links? Be specific as if you are writing a play script

   What exact thought (or belief), feeling or action followed the precipitating event?

   Look at each link – was there an alternative feeling or action that could have happened?

5. What are the consequences of this behaviour? Be specific

   How did others react immediately and later?

   How did you feel immediately and later?

   What effect did the behaviour have on you and your environment?

6. Describe in detail different solutions to the problem

   Go back to the chain and identify every point/link where if you had acted differently you would have avoided problem behaviour

   Identify what alternative actions you could have taken

   What coping behaviours or skilful behaviours could you have utilised?

7. Describe in detail the prevention strategy

   How could you have reduced your vulnerability to the chain?

   How could you have prevented the chain from starting?

   What would need to be in place to avoid a chain in the future?

8. Describe what actions are needed to repair the consequences of the problem behaviour

   Who else was hurt by the behaviour?

   What actions might you take to make reparation?

Figure 7.5 Working through a behaviour chain analysis

✓ **Aims**

- To increase understanding of a problem behaviour in a family to develop an effective intervention or solution.

- To support the client towards a first step in problem-solving – understanding what needs to change.

- To identify vulnerabilities and risks.

- To have opportunities to validate feelings.

👍 **Handy hints**

Not everyone will embrace the chain analysis, but do try not to be sidetracked. It can be a helpful way of responding to a maladaptive strategy or behaviour (e.g. self-harm, parasuicide or drug use) in a way that shows interest but avoids reinforcing the behaviour. It also links well with activities in Chapter 9 around capacity and motivation for change.

CHAPTER 8

WHAT'S THE PROBLEM?
Exploring Risks and Needs

Considering what we know about the impact of trauma on our capacity to talk about difficult things and of the shame associated with asking for help for some individuals and communities, it is unsurprising that for many practitioners the most challenging aspect of assessing vulnerable children and their families is exploring risks and needs. Of course, in the context of assessment, many parents and carers already know aspects of their behaviour (e.g. drug use, self-harm or offending) may be judged to be harmful to their child, and this further complicates the issue. Parents/carers may perceive or anticipate that professionals will be blaming, punishing or even threatening, especially in safeguarding contexts where the stakes are so high. One of the key messages from research is for practitioners to prioritise building trusting relationships with vulnerable families. 'It is therefore necessary that parents and children feel that they are not stigmatised when seeking help and that they retain an appropriate degree of control over subsequent stages of the support and protection process' (Thoburn *et al.* 2009, p.1).

When it comes to exploring risks and needs it is imperative if we are to work *with* complex families, that we are transparent about our purpose from the start. Clarity around our concerns and awareness of the importance of having focus in our assessment sessions, specifically around those issues that may be contributing to any harm to a child, is critical. It's not always enough to ask just once and accept the response given; we sometimes need to be prepared to keep asking difficult questions, respectfully and without judgement. Parents who either don't wish to or cannot address an addiction problem or who are aware that their partner's violence is harmful to their child may be too afraid of the consequences to be honest about the problems or to seek support for fear of being perceived as having failed in their parenting task. Parents with ongoing significant mental health or physical health needs may similarly worry that any contact with statutory services may result in their child coming into care (Thoburn *et al.* 2009). These issues can serve as major barriers to engagement and can be very difficult to disclose or talk about in an assessment.

Clearly there are factors related to the practitioner's communication skills and creativity that help facilitate difficult conversations with children and their families that have already been explored (see Chapter 2) as well as building safety into relationships (see Chapter 1). That said, some parents and caregivers, who perhaps because of their own relational trauma or mental ill health will be unable to establish a collaborative working relationship, may feel they need to withhold information or not be honest with you about the risks. A consistent offer of high support as well as high challenge is essential in these contexts, together with robust, multi-agency communication.

In the Good Lives Model (G-map, 2016, p.96) they use the concept of an *honesty line* in the early stages of their work with young people who sexually harm others. They talk about the diverse constraints on being honest, including wanting to create a positive impression or feeling reluctant to disclose embarrassing information. When you are exploring areas of concern, risk or need, or issues that are especially sensitive, you can ask, 'Where are you on the honesty line when you're talking about…?' This allows you to acknowledge the material is challenging or complex and that as such it might be hard for him to be entirely open and honest. The goal is for the person to give honesty ratings of 10 consistently.

Figure 8.1 Honesty line

In social work, exploration of risks and needs must relate to the three interconnected domains of the Assessment Framework (DoH 2000: the child's development; parenting capacity; and family and environmental factors. It is likely that a combination of these factors is interacting to lead to family stressors. Adapting a technique from non-violent resistance (Omer 2004) can be helpful here, where the concept of baskets helps parents/carers prioritise what behaviours to focus on first and what to ignore for now. You can use this same principle to think about worries, needs or risks with families.

Explain to the parent that he has three baskets; they can be real, imagined or illustrated baskets.

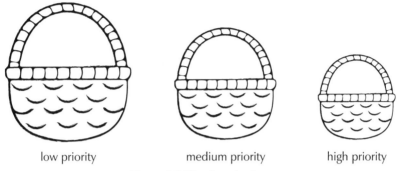

low priority   medium priority   high priority

Figure 8.2 The three baskets

Ask the parent to write all the issues and concerns that are live in his family system right now on small pieces of paper or post-it notes. Then take this pile of issues and ask him to prioritise them honestly. Examples might be:

- son (13) not coming in on time at night

- rent arrears

- outstanding repairs to the home

- violent arguments between parents

- daughter (15) refusing to go to school – hasn't got the correct uniform

- paternal grandmother with dementia and needing lots of additional care from family members

- mother with agoraphobia and unable to leave the house for the last three months

- father drinking alcohol daily – at least five cans of strong lager.

In the small basket, he needs to place the most critical things that he thinks really must be dealt with as a priority; because it is small, he can only put one or two things in to deal with at once. Then into the medium basket goes everything he feels he needs to tackle next (or as and when) and in the big basket, put all those things that are the least concerning. It doesn't mean the things in the medium and large baskets are not important, simply that they are not a priority at that moment.

This can have the effect of reducing the pressure parents/caregivers feel when they believe they must deal with every issue in one fell swoop. Instead you can use this technique to figure out where to start. The idea is to revisit the baskets as the parent/carer begins to make some progress with the small basket items and re-prioritise. Of course, in an ideal world the small basket, high-priority items will be the same for the practitioner as they are for parent/carer. Where there are clear discrepancies, this is useful information both to inform your risk assessment and to help engage the parent.

Another option to assist with the identification of risks and needs from a parent/carer perspective would be to have a list of areas relating to self, partner or individual children in the family such as:

- health

- emotional and social development

- behaviour

- identity and self esteem

- family and social relationships

- self-care and independence

- learning or education and employment

- achievements and aspirations

- impact of parenting

- impact of wider family or environmental factors.

You then ask the parent/carer to rate the level of concern for each area using a traffic light system: Green represents no concern; Amber some concern; and Red high concern. Red concerns are the equivalent of small-basket items (adapted from Blackpool Council Family Assessment Tool in Kendall, Rodger and Palmer 2010).

In this chapter you will find creative techniques to explore worries, risks or unmet needs in family systems, particularly focusing on parenting capacity. Remember that in your analysis you will need to be balancing strengths against those identified needs (see Chapter 3). If it's safe to do so, you might want to begin with thinking about the child's or family's priorities. What do they want help with or wish to discuss, bearing in mind that we are often supporting families with complex needs? What would the parent/carer's priority be versus the child's priority? This could be, for example, housing, poverty, debt, child behaviour, mental or physical health concerns.

REFRAMING

Materials

Paper and drawing materials.

Process

If you are working with someone who has experienced a stressful event or is experiencing a relationship as difficult (either a child or an adult), this is a good exercise for looking at the situation from different perspectives. You can use this technique to consider a specific incident (e.g. child on parent violence or a parent leaving a young child home alone) or a relationship (tensions between adolescent and parent or coercive control in a consenting adult relationship).

On one piece of paper ask the person to illustrate or map out the stressful situation or relationship. He can use words, symbols, shapes or a literal representation. On a second sheet of paper have some glasses – or with children and young people, you could even have some toy spectacles/comedy glasses to act this part out. These glasses are used to see the perspective of others; for example, how would someone the person respected view this situation? Ideally this person will be someone whose opinion is valued. Compare these different perspectives, viewing the situation through a different or wider lens. If this person was in the same situation as you find yourself, how might he respond? What might he be thinking or feeling? Notice whether there are similarities or differences in the responses.

✓ Aims

- To validate strong and difficult feelings, which is important in terms of getting alongside and building a collaborative relationship.

- To increase the person's insight and perspective and empathy for self.

- To consider coping skills and the capacity to imagine different outcomes or possibilities

👍 Handy hints

You can also do a similar activity with couples, siblings or family groups. It is worth remembering however that children under the age of eight or nine will typically not have the capacity developmentally to integrate multiple perspectives on a story.

This is a great opportunity to consider an individual's capacity for empathy for self and others and to understand how different family members might be experiencing the stressor or the 'problem'. You could for example explore the impact of one parent's mental health or alcohol use on the family system or on a couple relationship. You could explore the impact of a child's complex health needs or disability on other siblings in the family or upon the parenting relationship.

EXTERNALISING THE PROBLEM

✂ Materials

Pen and paper.

✎ Process

Externalising a problem or behaviour can be a useful way of exploring issues with children and young people without apportioning blame or shame; the method was developed in the family therapy field by Michael White in the 1980s. I use this technique most commonly with issues such as anxiety, soiling or angry outbursts. The first step is to identify a name for the problem, using the language of the child. In my work, I've found that it's important that what gets externalised is named in a way that fits well for the person concerned, so take your time with this and don't impose your own understanding or interpretation.

> This is because once a name is found for the problem that is close to the person's experience, it means that the skills and ideas of the person concerned become more available. For instance, it is very hard for a kid to think they have anything to offer in dealing with all the trouble that seems to be surrounding them – but dealing with Mr Mischief is another matter! (Carey and Russell 2002)

Sometimes younger children like the name to begin with Mr or Mrs. For example, a child I worked with who struggled with regulation called it Mrs Meltdown, therefore avoiding the shaming of talking of *her* 'meltdowns'. It can be helpful to ask the child to draw or describe the 'character'. Also ask, 'What does she sound like, smell like, do or think?' Then you can map the scope and influence of the problem – include the positives and make sure your language isn't deterministic. The problem cannot cause or make a person do something, rather it influences, invites, tells, tricks, tries to convince, etc.

For example, you can ask:

- When *Mrs Meltdown* visits, what does she do?

- How is it in your family when *she* is asleep or on holiday?

- How do you know when *she* is coming to visit?

- Who else notices when *she* is nearby?

Then look to identify alternative narratives or the start of a new story or understanding of the difficulty.

- Can you think of times when *Mrs Meltdown* nearly sneaked in, but you kept her out?

- Can you think of times when you would have thought *she* would come and stay but didn't?

- How did you get *her* to stay away?

- What does that say about how much stronger you are than *Mrs Meltdown*?

- Can anyone help you when you think *Mrs Meltdown* might be close?

- When has *Mrs Meltdown* whispered in your ear and you ignored her?

If possible, build on the new story projecting into the future.

- How do you think life without *Mrs Meltdown* is going to be?

- Who will notice in three, six or 12 months' time if *Mrs Meltdown* is still gone?

- What qualities do you have that means you can stand up to *Mrs Meltdown's* plans for you?

✓ Aims

- To introduce playfulness and humour into a potentially difficult situation.

- To allow for exploration of a problem or a worry through personification, allowing children to see they are not the problem – the problem is the problem.

- To allow for deeper exploration of how the problem has come to have so much influence in the person's life.

👍 Handy hints

An extension to this activity is to think about whether the child can enlist someone onto his 'team' to beat the problem. For assessment purposes, it will be interesting to see if there is anyone in this child's network he can rely on for help (see Identifying Personal Networks in Chapter 3).

Alternatively, you could introduce a doll, teddy or puppet, particularly for a younger child. This 'friend' can be identified as someone who has similar difficulties to the child or who may live in a similar context. This is another form of externalising the situation/problem, so the child can feel more in control and potentially also less exposed by your questions. You can also ask different kinds of questions when you have a third object in the session and will often find that children will offer their own thoughts, feelings and experiences through the 'friend'.

Here are some examples, if we imagine the friend is a dog puppet called Jake.

- How do you think Jake and Mrs Meltdown get along with each other?

- Why do you think Mrs Meltdown visits Jake?

- What is it like in Jake's family when Mrs Meltdown visits?

- Who would notice in Jake's family if Mrs Meltdown was around and what would they say about her?

- How does Jake show his feelings about Mrs Meltdown?

- Have you been able to help Jake beat Mrs Meltdown? How did you help him? What did you suggest? How did you know to come up with such a good idea?

- Are you pleased that Jake can sometimes do so well and stop Mrs Meltdown from coming?

This technique is not limited to use with children either. If an adult describes himself in negative terms (e.g. 'I'm useless') or when he is impacted by a mental health issue or substance misuse, for example, then these are also opportunities for externalisation. You can see this as an opportunity to ask questions that will lead to externalised conversations around these identity markers or definitions of self. Equally valid when you are working with the alternative stories of people's lives and someone mentions an inherent character trait ('My bravery helps me carry on' or 'I never give up') is to take the opportunity to have an externalising conversation. This can lead to a richer understanding of that particular aspect of the person and offer opportunities to link in with other skills and knowledge.

Remember that externalising conversations should be flexible and creative; they are also ongoing. It is not an option to use externalising language one week in an assessment session and then use internalising language the next. It is also relevant to mention that there doesn't have to be only one externalised definition of the problem. When working with different family members, it is quite likely that there will be more than one definition, but this does not preclude individuals from coming together to address the issues.

WORRY TREE

✂ Materials
Drawing paper, pens/pencils (leaf shapes, glue – optional).

✏ Process
Ask the child to draw a tree (or provide a tree outline if you think this might be too difficult). Then suggest he represent his worries on the tree. You could provide printed leaf shapes for the child to write his worries on and stick them on the tree. If you don't have time for this or if you have a creative child you might suggest he represents his worries using symbols, words, colours or drawings. Then think together about the kind of tree that has been drawn; its height, roots, stability, amount of leaves, etc. You can also begin to unpick the child's fears or worries and work together to find solutions or ways to manage them.

✓ Aims

– To allow the individual to express worries or concerns.

– To explore what is needed to address the worries and allow him to feel safe.

👍 Handy hints
Another helpful tool for children who have fears, or anxieties is the book *The Huge Bag of Worries* (Ironside 2004). I often read this story with younger children and encourage them to create their own bag of worries.

Rather than a Worry Tree, you could also make a Worry Bee, where each worry is drawn as a stripe on a bumble bee.

BUILDING STRONG WALLS

✂ Materials
Paper or post-it notes, pens, scissors (optional – building blocks).

Process

This is an exercise adapted from *Life Story Books for Adopted Children* by Joy Rees (2017). It can be used with adults or children but for the purposes of explanation, I'll assume you are working with a child. Ask him to think about all the different things that parents need to do to look after their children and keep them safe. Tell him that bringing up children is a bit like building a wall, and to build a strong wall, all the right bricks must be in place. Describe the foundations and the cement as being the love that the parent has for the child, but also explore what else children need from their parents.

If you are using paper, cut out rectangles to look like bricks or use post-it notes and write the child's needs on them. Stick them together to form a wall, with the foundations (the parent's love for the child) already drawn. If you have building blocks, write the child's needs on pieces of paper or post-it notes, stick them on the blocks and build a wall together. You need the wall to include: providing nurture and physical affection; meeting the child's health and physical needs; providing rules, supervision and boundaries and a safe environment; and the need for fun, play and laughter.

Figure 8.3 Example of Building Strong Walls

When you have finished, you can wonder what might happen if some of the bricks were missing from the wall. If you have used building blocks you can encourage the child to take or push a brick or two out to see what happens, for example if there isn't always food for the child or boundaries and safety. The important message here is that parents consistently need to do all these things for the child, or the wall becomes too wobbly and can fall down. If the parent can't build a strong enough wall, then the child won't grow up to be safe, healthy and happy.

If you think the child can manage such a direct discussion you can end the exercise by making links with the child's own situation and the worries that have prompted the assessment. Reflect that even with the strong foundations of love, parents sometimes struggle to do all the things children need. The idea that love is a mixture of what is said and what is done by the parent is important. Try to be honest in your explanations of what is going 'wrong' in respect of the child's parenting experience without using too many euphemisms or oversimplifications that can leave the child confused. For example, if the child's basic care needs are not being met because both parents are using heroin, don't say 'Your mummy and daddy are poorly.' The child will need a truthful but compassionate and age-appropriate explanation.

✓ Aims

- To use a creative method that begins in a more general way to discuss a child's basic needs and can become as personal as you feel is appropriate for the child.

- To help the child understand any worries about unmet need.

- To learn more about whether the child's basic needs are being met day to day.

👍 Handy hints

In my experience this is a powerful exercise whether you make direct links with the child's own experience or not. Many children will make their own links with their current experiences of being parented and may need your support to manage this; it can be painful to acknowledge that your wall is 'wobbly'.

It is important to emphasise that *all* children need the right sort of care from parents and it is the parent's job to provide it. There is nothing the child can do to change things or make his parents better able to care for him. Stress that he is a special person who deserves a family and a home to grow up in where he will be loved, safe and protected (Melville 2005).

An alternative to this activity is to have a baby doll and have a conversation with the child about what this baby might need. You can ask the child to imagine what he might do if the baby was crying and act this out together. Discuss the need for warmth, food, love, nappy changing, fun and safety, etc. You might consider the baby's changing needs as he gets older and starts to crawl and walk. This is an opportunity to talk about what a parent's job is, in whatever detail is appropriate.

Ensure you focus as much on the non-functional aspects of care, like cuddles, kisses and play, as many children will simply focus on the very practical aspects of parenting, like feeding and clothing. For the child who carries a sense of blame that he is in some way responsible for not being cared for properly, this activity can underline the universal needs of small children and that babies are not 'bad' for crying and needing a parent's attention.

This is also an exercise that can be useful with parents who would respond better to a more active method of engagement to help explore whether they have a good understanding of the complexities of the parenting role.

THE PARENTING GAME

✂ Materials

Four boxes with letterbox holes (one large enough to fit the other three inside) and 'three parent model' laminated cards as described below.

✏ Process

Fahlberg (1991) was the first to write about the three-part parenting model and others (Nicholls 2005; Ryan and Walker 2007) have followed. Nicholls developed a game which, in life story work, helps the child understand the complexities of parenting, but in assessments can be used for people of all ages, including adults, to look at whether parenting is good enough and how children perceive their experience of being parented. What follows is my interpretation of this game.

Take four boxes, making sure one of them is large enough to fit the other three inside. Label the largest box BEING A PARENT, and the remaining boxes BORN TO PART, PARENTING PART and LEGAL PART. It's fine to adapt these names if you think of something more suitable for the child or parent you're working with. I have a set of laminated, re-usable cards that read as follows and try to capture many aspects of the role of parents, but of course this is not an exhaustive list:

BORN TO PART

- the colour of your eyes, hair, skin
- the way you look – the shape of your face, mouth and nose
- your build, frame and height
- how clever you could be
- the size of your feet, hands and ears
- the sort of personality you have – are you shy, chatty or funny?
- what you're good at; this might be art, playing an instrument or a sport
- what illnesses you might get

PARENTING PART

- keeps you safe from harm
- makes you feel good about yourself

- helps with homework and learning new skills – like using a knife and fork or riding a bike

- takes you out to different places to have fun

- makes sure you have clothes, toys and books

- ensures you have a clean, warm, safe home to live in

- loves you no matter what

- takes you to school or nursery when you are old enough

- takes you to the doctor or dentist

- gives you good food to help you grow and keep you healthy

- teaches you what is wrong and right

- gives you hugs or cuddles

- plays and talks with you

LEGAL PART

- decides on your name and registers your birth

- gives permission for you to stay overnight or go on holiday with family or friends

- decides what immunisations you should have

- gives permission for you to go on school trips

- gives permission for medical treatment

- chooses what religion you follow

- chooses your school and makes sure you go every day

You then have a number of options, but first talk about the three parts to being a parent: the born to part that makes us what we are; the parenting part that looks after us and makes sure we are safe and well; and the legal part that makes big decisions for us now and in the future. Stress that all these things make up being a parent and parents have to do them all at once and all of the time (Nicholls 2005). Explain to the child that being a parent to any child can be a difficult job because there are so many things to remember to do to make sure the child is safe, happy and healthy. They can't just do these things for some of the time; they have to do them until the child is grown up and able to take care of himself.

One option is to explore with the child or young person which cards belong in which box. Then put the smaller three boxes inside the larger BEING A PARENT box. Alternatively, you can put the cards in the right boxes yourself and then encourage the child to take the cards out of the smaller boxes, looking at them and talking about them together one at a time. As each card is discussed, ask the child to post it back into the large box. With both options, when all the cards have been posted, ask the child to give the box a good shake and refer to how parents must juggle all these tasks at once. Often in vulnerable families, it is the parenting part of the task that brings the greatest challenges.

There are lots of opportunities potentially within this game for hearing about the child's lived experience of being parented and his expectations of what this might mean for him. You can also do this exercise with parents and caregivers.

✓ Aims

- To understand the child's experiences of being parented.

- To begin to identify unmet need as well as strengths within the parenting system.

It is possible to use this game to help you explain why you might be involved with the family if it has already been identified that there are weaknesses in one or more of the parenting parts; for example, if the child is not attending school regularly or the child may not be adequately supervised in light of his age and developmental stage. This would be appropriate both for children and for some parents too.

👍 Handy hints
If you are working with a parent or carer with a learning disability, or who is a more visual learner, you can use this exercise to explore parenting capacity. Rather than just having words on the card, you could use illustrative pictures, which helps engage

younger children, those who are not confident readers or who have English as a second language.

Tait and Wosu (2016) describe a similar activity they call 'Maslow's boxes', which they used to help a mother understand the impact of neglect on her child. It can also be used to help assess a parent's ability to care for a child safely. You need seven lidded boxes, each a little smaller than the other so you can stack them in a pyramid, and labelled with one of Maslow's identified needs (Maslow 1943):

- being all you can be (self-actualisation)

- beauty, nature, balance, order and form (aesthetic needs)

- knowledge, understanding, exploration, curiosity (cognitive needs)

- respect for self and others, feeling competent, self-esteem (esteem needs)

- receiving and giving love, affection, trust, acceptance (need for love and belonging)

- protection from danger, feeling safe (safety needs)

- basic needs like food, drink, somewhere to live (physical needs) – this is the biggest box, which sits at the base of the pyramid.

Figure 8.4 Maslow's Hierarchy of Needs (1943)

Explain that the exercise is about exploring everything a human being needs; you can do this with a parent or family group. Starting with the biggest box you invite the family to write all their physical needs on little slips of paper and pop them in the box. It really helps to personalise your prompts, for example:

- So, what do you think your baby needs?

- How is that different from your teenager?

- Who met your physical needs when you were little?

Repeat this with each of the boxes and start to build a pyramid or a tower with the completed boxes. For assessment purposes, notice which were the easier and harder boxes to fill. Did the adults and children have similar ideas or expectations? When your tower is complete you can simply explain Maslow's theory to parents and carers that if one need wasn't met at the right time, in the child's time frame, the next need in the pyramid couldn't be well met, and a child's developmental trajectory will be compromised. You can keep this relevant to the family's own circumstances by giving specific examples if you have them. For example, explaining that a child's physical needs are not being fully met if he is sleeping on a mattress with no bedding in a cold house, because his parent hasn't got enough money to buy an electricity token. This can be a really helpful tool in being explicit about the worries you have, which is the only way a parent/carer will be clear about what needs to change.

With some parents you might ask them to pull out the bottom box, which represents fundamental basic physical needs and which will see the pyramid collapse. Again, this can be a useful illustration for some parents/carers of what is happening to their own child's development. Tait and Wosu (2016, p.100) comment on how 'it is a hard message to give and, being visual, it often touches people in a way words don't. Distress can be a catalyst for change, so if the client is upset allow this to happen. Don't try to comfort too soon.'

If possible, you would wish then to move on to thinking about what is needed to build the pyramid back up. Depending on the gravity of the situation for the child, you might also need to talk about the possible outcomes if the child's basic needs remain unmet. You can use the exercise Building Strong Walls earlier in this chapter to similar effect.

THE NEEDS JIGSAW

Materials

The Needs Jigsaw – a wooden, colourful jigsaw of a child. Each piece of the jigsaw represents a different need (e.g. food, cleanliness and hygiene, education, time and patience, fun, responsibility, identity, guidance and good examples). There are accompanying header cards that can provide prompts before and during a session.

A newer version The Needs Jigsaw II was developed in response to practitioners who wanted an alternative jigsaw to use with older children or young parents. The needs in this jigsaw are more suited to the needs of young people and adults; for example, equality, rest, safety and protection, choices/control, praise and encouragement, interested and reliable adults, friendships, understanding/empathy.

They can be ordered at www.familyworkresources.co.uk/needs-jigsaw.html.

Process

The tool was developed by Kathy Stevens, a social worker in early years in West Yorkshire in 1994. It is designed to be non-threatening and simple with high visual impact. When the jigsaw is complete, it represents a visual representation of the 'whole child'. Missing jigsaw pieces represent gaps in the child's development and can help you to have discussions about unmet needs with parents. You will work with the parent to put the wooden jigsaw pieces together. Doing so can help build rapport, promote discussion about the different needs of children and provide insight potentially for both parent and practitioner into those needs. Parents/carers will need a clear explanation of the purpose of the exercise, that it isn't a 'test' but a tool to explore their understanding and knowledge of what all children need. It can help practitioners assess what additional support, if any, might be required.

So, to get started place the pieces face down on the table and ask parents to choose a 'need'. You can then ask questions from the prompt cards that are relevant to your assessment to generate discussion and identify strengths in understanding of their child's needs as well as potential gaps. Its interactive focus takes away some of the pressure of a typical verbal question–answer exchange and can form a good basis for engagement.

✓ Aims

- To enhance communication, especially with adults with learning disabilities or younger parents during assessments of parenting capacity.

- To demonstrate to parents that all the child's needs must be met for children to develop healthily and safely to meet their potential.

👍 Handy hints

If you can't get hold of the original jigsaw or cost is prohibitive, you can make your own. Either design your own jigsaw child on card and laminate it for future use, or ask the parent to draw himself on a piece of paper and divide the drawing into six parts. Make a list together of all things that might be important to him – his needs. This could include food, friends, shelter, education, an income, peace, no discrimination, good health, etc. Then ask him to choose six rights from the list that would be considered important now, which will be written on the jigsaw pieces. Can he identify rights that are fundamental to every person? Can he identify rights that would be fundamental to his child/children?

Another option is to use child need cards. You can buy a pack or make your own. A great resource is *Kids Need...: Parenting Cards for Families and the People Who Work with Them* (Hamer 2007). Each card features a child's need, such as fresh fruit and vegetables, pocket money, their own bedroom. You then invite the participant to place the cards in one of three categories: Kids Need; Kids Sometimes Need; and Kids Don't Need. The use of pictures and symbols mean they are great for parents who have difficulty reading or who have English as a second language.

CHAPTER 9

ASSESSING CHANGE FACTORS

In social work terms it is not only vital that we are assessing whether a child has come to harm and what caused it, but also what can be done to improve the current family situation. This therefore necessitates consideration of whether parents or carers can make sufficient changes in the child's timeframe to ensure the child's needs are met *and* that he will be safe now and in the future. So how do we consider changes that will benefit the child? Whatever the change model, it is vital to acknowledge that different people will be at different stages of readiness to change and can move between those stages at different rates. We cannot assume that people are ready for, or indeed desire to make, immediate or permanent behaviour, parenting or lifestyle changes simply because others deem them to be necessary.

It is only by identifying the individual's position in terms of a change process that we will be able to match our planning and intervention to his inclination, capacity and readiness. We need to understand whether people have both the capacity – the Intelligence Quotient (IQ), Emotional Quotient (EQ) or emotional intelligence, resources and support – and the motivation to change – the desire, the hope for a better future, a belief that what is being offered will help provide the answer. If the practitioner is the only one that is worried about a problem, positive change within a family system is unlikely. It is important to understand how the individual understands the problem and what ownership he has of it, as well as thinking about the functional nature of the 'problem' or the behaviour. Change, after all 'affects more than just behaviour; it affects a person's identity, esteem, control, confidence and sense of belonging' (Morrison 2010, p.308).

In terms of theory, we have been somewhat limited in social work in the UK to the Transtheoretical or Stages of Change model. Although this work from Prochaska and DiClemente (1982) is over 30 years old and was developed in relation to substance use and dependence, it remains well used in contemporary practice, with some limitations, particularly in the child protection arena with families who have not always chosen to seek help to change. Baynes (2015, p.34) suggests that the model fails to 'take account of the strong incentive for favourable self-representation inherent within the child-protection context'. This is significant within a process that takes a verbal expression of commitment to change as an indicator that change will then follow. She also raises the important issue of the labelling of parents/carers who deny the need for support or reject the need for change as 'pre-contemplative', 'in denial' or 'resistant', because this fails to recognise pressures on parents to deny risks or concerns for fear of what action may follow (Baynes, 2015).

Ultimately change can be difficult for us all, but it is eminently more challenging for families where there are other factors at play that increase the risk of harm or recurrence of harm, such as domestic abuse, poor mental health, and substance misuse, alongside environmental factors like poverty, unemployment or insecure housing. In this context, we must consider the power differential and pressure on parents/carers to present themselves more positively. There will always be the risk of coercion in statutory interventions with families, but we should acknowledge that we then risk ambivalent parents/carers becoming harder still to reach. It is vital that we consider the different factors that promote or inhibit parental engagement and link this to the concept of *disguised compliance* or *resistance* (see Introduction).

Stanley, Cleaver and Hart (2010) explore the idea of parents' 'hidden needs' such as substance misuse, mental health difficulties and domestic violence. These needs carry such social stigma, more so in certain communities than others, that people will go to great lengths to hide or minimise their struggles, and this inevitably impacts change. They also share a body of evidence relating to an over-focus on mothers in safeguarding, irrespective of where the problem is located within the system. This gender bias can also negatively impact on the engagement of women, who can feel scapegoated or under scrutiny, and on men who are frequently absent from assessments.

Models of change

Stages of Change model

As the model is still widely utilised in the UK, let's consider Prochaska and DiClemente's model in more detail. It has, as a basic premise, that change is a matter of balance; so, people will only change their behaviour when the motivational forces for change are higher than those in favour of things staying the same. For the change process to be effective, the practitioner must first assess which stage in the model the client has reached in terms of readiness to accept or deny the need for change.

Figure 9.1 Stages of Change model
(adapted from Prochaska and DiClemente 1982)

The logical starting point for the model is *Pre-contemplation*. At this stage, the individual may not be aware a problem even exists and is unlikely therefore to have an intention to change his behaviour. The benefits or positives of maintaining the behaviour outweigh the negatives or any adverse consequences. Parents/carers at this stage are unable to make a full commitment to change as they haven't accepted the need to. Commitment or perceived motivation may therefore be tokenistic or unrealistic, such as, 'I'll do whatever you say.'

At the *Contemplation* stage, the person becomes aware that there is a problem but may still have ambivalent feelings about taking the next step. An individual can dwell in the contemplation stage of change for long periods of time; he has not yet made a commitment to change but may be becoming more aware of some of the adverse consequences of things remaining the same (legal, social, emotional, physical, etc.). The assessment process is an essential tool in facilitating this stage; however, be aware that the time the adult needs in contemplation may be incompatible with the child's needs or the timescale for the assessment.

A shift in thinking occurs at the *Preparation* (or *Determination*) stage when the person commits to making positive changes. In order for this to happen he needs to 'buy in' to the idea that the change is a good thing and must also have a sense of self-efficacy: he must believe he can make changes and can influence the future. Although he may be taking some small steps towards change, at this point, he may ultimately decide *not* to do anything to change his behaviour. In this phase of the cycle, it can be helpful to be explicit in an agreement for work towards change, including the specifics of who will do what, when and how. There must be no doubt in a parent/carer's mind about what he is expected to do to meet his child's needs.

It is, however, not until the *Action* stage that the person is in an active phase of change and where behaviour begins to be discernibly different. He may experiment with different strategies for achieving change and is likely to remain ambivalent on some level. Changes may be behavioural or environmental and may include attempting to use support and services offered to him. However, for any changes to be sustained and for new behaviours to replace old behaviours, the individual must move into the *Maintenance* stage. Emphasis here is on consolidation of changes, through rehearsal, testing out new skills and healthy coping strategies over time and in different contexts.

During this phase he may be at risk of *Relapse* and could fall back into old behaviours or patterns of relating. Each time the individual travels through the cycle he should learn from each relapse and hopefully grow stronger and more committed to positive change, so each relapse is shorter or has a less negative impact. This is known as the *upward spiral*. It is important when supporting people through this cycle to acknowledge relapses as opportunities for learning and building on the resolve to change. Minimising the risk of relapse involves a partnership between the parent/carer and worker to look at strategies to manage unpredictable or unforeseen stressors that are part of everyday life.

This is not a linear model but a process that can be applied across all social care settings and can be helpfully shared with families too. There are lots of Stages of Change handouts available that are free to download, so you can use them to support clients to identify where they are; it also supports you to work from a strengths-based perspective. Conceptualising change as a stage process can help everyone see shifts along a continuum and track progress.

Seven Steps to Determination

An alternative is the Seven Steps to Determination model (in Leeds City Council's Practitioner Assessment Resource Pack), which is another visual prompt for use with families, focusing on motivation to change. You can use the analogy of climbing a ladder or flight of stairs as this can help in assessing whether the motivational factors can outweigh the status quo. If not, change is unlikely to occur.

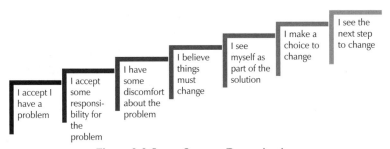

Figure 9.2 Seven Steps to Determination

Working towards change

Whichever model is followed, the first step to change is to agree on the problem. This is much easier said than done, especially if social work services are involved, which may leave people acutely aware of the power imbalance and feeling coerced into changing behaviours rather than making an active choice. A degree of ambivalence is understandable, where people have developed adaptive strategies to help themselves to manage in everyday life. If at this point change is forced through with the focus on external agents of change, it is unlikely to be sustained once the external factors are removed.

To help people accept responsibility for the problem you need to elicit some change talk. There may of course remain a high level of ambivalence or resistance, but you can see a slight shift in perspective and some expression of participation or involvement in the problem. The next step of moving beyond complacency or immobilisation/powerlessness towards action is a challenge. For as long as it feels easier or inevitable for things to stay as they are, finding the energy, motivation or inspiration to begin to do things differently can represent a significant challenge. People need to feel that they can't tolerate or live with this problem any longer to tap into the will power and motivation to believe things must change, and then act.

At this point it is not unusual for people to still feel powerless to influence their lives, relying instead on being 'rescued' from the distress and pain they're experiencing. It can be a challenge for the worker at this stage to maintain a restorative focus of working *with* the service user and not doing *to* or *for*. When we work alongside people at times of challenge to resolve difficulties and make reparation where there has been harm, there is strong evidence to suggest that outcomes for children and their families improve. People are understandably happier, more cooperative and likely to make positive changes when people in perceived positions of power or authority work with them in this way. Be mindful of the Social Discipline Window; to be working restoratively we need to be in the top right square: the **WITH** box with equal measure of high support and high challenge.

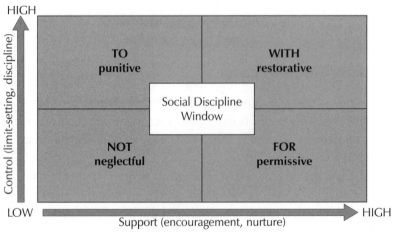

Figure 9.3 Social Discipline Window
(adapted from Wachtel 2016)

The person must see himself as part of the solution; this can trigger new behaviours and helps challenge negative self-talk or internal thought patterns; for example, 'There's no point trying, because nothing will be any different' or 'What's the point? It won't last.'

You should be working with the person to generate several different strategies or approaches that will support him to make changes in his behaviour. Some will be practical, but most will require sustained action on the part of the individual as opposed to earlier talk or beliefs that would have put the emphasis on actions by others. It can help to rehearse or practice some of these actions or strategies, because often support is needed to move into action.

One would expect that after the first step is taken there should be a payoff; an impact or lessening of the pressure, distress or discomfort. This can be highly rewarding and a motivator to encourage the person to keep going. Change is of course an ongoing process and it's important to identify next steps to maintain the momentum of progress.

It is worth remembering that there are no time-specific parameters to change. Some people will be ready to move very quickly through the stages, whilst others will get 'stuck'. This is the time to explore the advantages and disadvantages of making changes and to think together about the possible consequences of choosing to make those changes or not. It is also helpful to note that people may be at different stages in the change cycle for different issues. For example, in the Contemplation stage for separating from a violent partner, but in the Pre-contemplation stage for reducing cannabis use. Having a good understanding of the Stages of Change model will help you explore appropriate support or interventions for children and families, identify barriers to positive change and provide you with opportunities to work with individuals to find ways to remove those barriers.

Motivational interviewing

In motivational interviewing (MI: Miller and Rollnick 2002), which also has its origins in the substance-misuse field, it is held that the behaviour of the practitioner can influence levels of resistance to change in the service user; yet another reminder of the relational aspect of assessment work. This goal-orientated counselling method operates on the principles of facilitating and engaging intrinsic motivation within the client to change behaviour. Resistance to change is not pathologised, but is absolutely recognised as an integral part of the process. It is important that in assessments we are also able to use skills to manage the fluctuations in an individual's motivation to make positive changes in his life.

There are four basic skills for the practitioner to master in MI. You must be able to ask open rather than closed questions that simply require a yes/no answer. You must be able to offer affirmations about the validity of the parent/carer's reality and reflexive listening. You will also be able to provide summary statements to the client. You'll do this while you focus on topics like looking at a typical day, looking back at previous life events and choices, looking forward and considering confidence about possible behaviour changes. Using summaries, preferably in partnership with the individual, can ensure learning points are made and tests understanding of a shared agreement. Throughout you must maintain a stance that is non-judgemental, non-confrontational and non-adversarial in order to elicit self-motivating statements that demonstrate an individual's capacity to make changes based on the skills or knowledge he has acquired.

It is important to think about the gains for the individual of maintaining the status quo. For example, when supporting a parent or caregiver who is using alcohol or substances, ask how this helps him cope? When working with a parent thinking about leaving a violent partner, ask what the greatest benefits to the relationship are. The qualities of empathic listening and validation are key as you also explore the disadvantages of following through with change. The change talk is always much more powerful coming from the service user, than when it is imposed by the worker.

Ambivalence about making changes is resolved by the client (not the worker) examining the pros and cons of change versus not changing. The idea of future pull can be helpful, where your dialogue helps create the idea of a better present and preferred future. Can you help the person become clearer in his mind about what he hopes for himself and others?

- How would life be different if X wasn't part of it?

- How does X get in the way of you doing what you'd like to do?

It can be helpful to think of a force field. What are the forces that push towards or pull away from a goal? Also effective is focusing discussion on how change has been achieved in the past. What were the driving and restraining forces and what helped him succeed? This focus on what has worked before, rather than what is going wrong now can be a helpful reframe and builds on the individual's sense of agency and efficacy. Baynes comments that 'this approach has changed the way that I talk with families; parents seem to feel better understood and these conversations help to hunt down even the faintest glimmer of motivation to change' (Baynes 2015, p.37).

The primary goals of MI are to engage the individual, elicit change talk and evoke motivation to make positive changes. Remember, though, that as with other change models, change talk, although a positive sign, is never evidence in and of itself that change will either be made or, even better, maintained. And thinking about change from a restorative practice perspective will keep your focus on making change plans *with* families and not making plans *for* them. Like learning any new behaviour, it is preferable to set limited, achievable goals initially, within a set timeframe, so children and families can have increased chance of success with small shifts in behaviour initially. This breeds confidence and self-esteem and increases the likelihood of success in tackling bigger challenges and change goals further down the line.

In this chapter you will find exercises that will support you to have conversations about change and to identify steps to change within the child's timeframe.

SCALING OR LIKERT SCALES

✂ Materials
Pen and paper or laminated cards numbered 1–10.

🖉 Process
Measuring change can be a key tool in encouraging more change in children, young people, their caregivers and the systems around families. When we begin to make progress, even the smallest steps can build confidence in our capacity to take control of an area of life and we will be likely to achieve more moving forward. Measuring or scaling questions can help establish a baseline before any intervention and help you know where to begin.

A standard and complete application of scaling questions contains the following steps. First explain the scaling question; this can be done as follows: Imagine a scale from 0 to 10. The 10 represents your desired situation/best case scenario. The 0 represents the situation in which nothing of that desired situation has yet been achieved. You could also sketch this scale out if a visual representation would work better.

Figure 9.4 A Likert scale

Ask about the current position.

Q. Where are you now on this scale?

Ask about what is already there. Focus on what there is between the 0 position and his current position.

Q. How did you manage to get to your current position on the scale?

Q. What has helped to get there? What worked well? What else has helped?

Offer encouragement and keep asking for more details until you get as full a description of what has helped reach this point. Ask about a past success. Ask about a situation previously where the individual has been a bit higher on the scale.

Q. Have you already been higher on the scale than your current position?

Q. What was the highest position you have been at on the scale?

Q. What was different, then? What did you do differently? What worked well?

Encourage him to visualise one step higher. Invite a description of what the situation will be like when the person is one step higher on the scale.

Q. What will one step higher on the scale look like?

Q. How will you notice you have reached one step higher on the scale?

Q. What will be different then?

Q. What will you be able to do then that you can't do now? Or what won't you be doing?

Ask about a small step forward. This encourages a sense of self-efficacy and agency.

Q. Has what we've discussed been helpful for you in choosing a step forward?

Q. What would you like that step be?

Q. What would need to happen for you to take that step?

Scaling questions are one of the most flexible of the solution-focused worker's tools and can be used in diverse ways, for example in working with a child:

Q. On a scale of 0–10, with 0 being the worst that things have been at home and 10 representing the best, where are you today?

Relatively few children answer this question with a 0. This immediately gives the worker the opportunity to ask:

Q. So, what is it that you are doing that means you are at… and not 0?

This question opens the way to identifying both pre-session change and expectations and represents an opportunity for goal-setting and identifying the possibility of change.

Q. So tell me how it will look when you are at an 8 or a 10.

In addition, it is a useful way of identifying the first small step that will demonstrate that change has happened or is occurring now:

Q. So if you are on 3 now, tell me what you will be doing when you are on 4?

Q. What will others notice about you? Your teacher? Your parent/carer?

Follow-up sessions can very quickly incorporate a view about change:

Q. Where are you today on the scale?

Q. So what have you done to move up two points?

Q. What are you doing differently?

Q. Even when things were difficult, how did you stop yourself from slipping back to…?

✓ Aims

- To assess hopefulness of change: has this person a sense of agency?

- To assess readiness or acceptance of the need for change.

- To consider whether individuals are able to identify small steps to change.

- To assess whether individuals have a realistic view of the situation – for example, if a family is being threatened with eviction for anti-social behaviour and yet scored relationships with neighbours as a 10, you might question either their honesty, their understanding of the situation or acceptance of the problem behaviours.

👍 Handy hints

This exercise can work well with younger children, adolescents and adults. With younger children you can choose visual representation of something the child likes (e.g. pictures of cars, sweets, footballs), but you would need to make sure you have 10 of each, or you could use a scale of 1–5 to simplify the exercise. Treisman (2017) also suggests that you could use different-sized LEGO® towers or balls of Playdoh/Plasticine to make this exercise more child-friendly.

If you are working in a larger space, it can be good to use laminated larger (A4) numbers. This way the numbers can be spread 0–10 across the room and you can ask the person to physically explore what it feels like to be on a 1, a 5 or a 10.

THE FUTURE SELF DRAWING

✂ Materials

Paper and drawing materials.

🖉 Process

This is an activity suggested by Blaustein and Kinniburgh (2010) in their chapter on self-development and identity as they feel it contributes to the development of a more coherent sense of self that integrates both past and present experiences. This activity can be used with people of different ages, but I will explain it from a child's perspective. The first step is to prompt the child to imagine himself in the future. Where will he be? What or who will he look like? Who might be with him? What will he be doing? Even with these questions, some children will have great difficulty imagining their future self, so you might need to ask very concrete questions like 'What do you think you would like to be when you grow up?'

Now ask the child to draw a picture of his imagined future self. Some children will prefer to describe the future in writing, others might want to write a poem or use song lyrics, all of which are good options too. Some may benefit from a prepared body outline to fill in or from using magazine images to make a collage if lacking confidence in their drawing abilities. You can then expand the concept if appropriate (usually with an older child, adolescent or adult to look at his capacity to imagine change) to imagine himself in five, ten and twenty years in the future. Either use three pieces of paper for this or fold one larger piece into three sections to represent increments of time. Work with the child to think about what steps he needs to take to achieve his five-, ten- and twenty-year goals. Try to identify external sources of support, such as parents and carers, teachers or sports coaches. What qualities does the child already possess that will help him reach his goals?

✓ Aims

– To build on the child's ability to imagine himself in the future and plan the bigger picture.

- To build connections between current actions and events and future outcomes by planning how to fulfil wishes and dreams.

- To build on the child's sense of having some control over his future by identifying what he has already achieved, what he wants to achieve and how he might achieve this goal.

👍 Handy hints

Geldard and Geldard (1997) suggest a similar timeline activity where you encourage the child to picture himself then, now and in the future. At each stage in the timeline you ask the child to write what he has achieved or what he would hope to achieve. Think with him about who or what he might need to help achieve these things.

Cavanagh Johnson (1998) comments that children who have grown up in chaotic households often learn to live in the moment and focus on survival rather than on long-term planning. These children are also less likely to have role models around them whom they would like to be like. She encourages children to think about when they grow up. She asks: 'What kind of person would you like to be?' or 'How would you like people to describe you in the future?' She then goes on to explore: 'Do you know anyone like this? What characteristics do they have and do they share any with you now?'

She might prompt the child with a list of characteristics or circumstances for the future that includes:

- have nice things

- do things for others

- be strong

- obey the law

- be kind to your children

- be a good friend

- have a good job

- admit when you get something wrong

- help others in trouble

- be generous

- get what you want without hurting others

- be loving

- care about your family.

Clearly this is not an exhaustive list but gives you an idea of how to prompt the child if necessary. She then asks the child to put a tick against how he would like things to be when grown up. Then he is asked to put another tick next to those things he thinks are the most important. She encourages the child to think of someone he knows with one of these characteristics and then to think of two concrete things he can do to achieve his goals.

MAKE A WISH

Materials

Paper, pens or crayons.

Process

There are three very simple options for this exercise, all of which are designed to explore the individual's hopes or wishes for the future; it is appropriate for use with children and adults. You can suggest either: making a wish as he pretends to blow away dandelion seeds; making a wish on a wishing well; or looking into a crystal ball and telling what he sees in the future. Geldard and Geldard (1997) suggest making a wish for today, tomorrow and for the future.

✓ Aims

- To encourage expression of hopes and dreams for the near and long-term future.

- To encourage the use of imagination and creativity.

- To identify whether the individual is holding on to unrealistic hopes and dreams about the future.

👍 **Handy hints**

Prepared images of a wishing well, crystal ball and dandelion can be found online or in 'anti-colouring books' for those who lack confidence in their drawing ability. It would also be simple to design your own worksheet using clip-art. Whilst it is great to encourage creativity and fantastical thinking in some cases, also be mindful of managing potentially unrealistic expectations of change.

Alternatively, you could use the *miracle question* taken from solution-focused therapy (De Shazer 2012) as a way to refocus the attention on a less problem-saturated story. There are various ways of using the miracle question. One idea is to encourage the person to write down or tell you in one sentence the (main) problem or issue from his perspective. Then ask, what if, while he was asleep tonight, a miracle happened and the problem was solved. When he wakes up tomorrow, he doesn't know that it's solved, but it has been… What would he be doing differently in the first few minutes? In the first few hours? For the rest of the day? You can extend this by asking him to draw or sculpt how things would look for him.

WALL OR TREE OF HOPE

✂ **Materials**

Felt-tip pens and paper – optional to have green card leaves already cut out or brick shapes/post-it notes.

✏ **Process**

When endeavouring to focus young people or parents/carers on strengths and goals for the future, this is a very simple exercise to support planning and to share hopes and dreams. It can also demonstrate whether individuals are able to project forward and imagine a different life for themselves, where positive change is possible.

There are two options here: one is to draw or make a tree and to have a series of leaf shapes for the individual to write on; the other is to use the idea of building a wall and either drawing a wall made of bricks or having a series of brick-shaped cards on which to write (post-it notes work well for this too). You then work to build a picture of what he hopes for his own or the family's future, exploring what might stay the same and what might change. Both adults and young people may need prompts with this if feeling very stuck or hopeless.

For an adolescent you might ask:

Where would you like to live? Would you live alone or have a partner or pet?

Would you be working or studying?

Would you like to travel?

For a parent you might ask:

Who would be supporting you?

What would help you manage pressure or stresses in life?

How would you see life for your children?

You might be able to extend this to think about what he needs to do to reach these goals.

✓ Aims

- To explore hopes and dreams for the future.

- To build on resilience and a sense of self-efficacy.

- To consider capacity for change.

Handy hints

You can also use this technique to explore things the individual would like to be better. Try to keep the focus pro-social – as in what they would like to see happen rather than what they want to stop. For example:

- For Mum and Dad to get along *not* For Mum and Dad to stop fighting

- To concentrate better at school *not* To stop getting detentions

- To be in a respectful, safe relationship *not* To get out of a violent relationship

WHAT'S YOUR ANCHOR?

✂ Materials

Paper and drawing materials.

✏ Process

This is an activity from Buchalter (2009) in which she suggests drawing your anchor – the thing that is keeping you from moving forward in your life. What is weighing you down? I find this most exercise most useful with adolescents or adult caregivers.

Use this opportunity to explore how long the anchor has been in the person's life. What does it look like; it's size, shape, colour, smell? What role is the anchor playing in restricting growth, movement or change? Is it always present? What purpose does it serve? What would life look like if the anchor were raised?

✓ Aims

- To explore restraining factors in achieving change, wellbeing or safety.

- To explore the person's interpretation of these 'blocks' and assess whether there is hope for or plans to achieve change.

- Where possible, to begin to work on identifying ways in which to 'break anchor'.

👍 Handy hints

Buchalter (2009) gives the example of an older woman who drew an anchor on the seabed, surrounded by sharks and other fish. She talked about not remembering a time without her anchor, which she felt stopped her from being part of the world and engaging in meaningful relationships. She identified her anchor as depression and insecurity, and the shark as her mother, circling with the negative statements and critical comments that she would hear regularly as a child. The fish were related to others in her life she felt had rejected her subsequently.

Other examples of interpretation of the anchor might be drug or alcohol dependency, an abusive relationship or difficulties with self-regulation (e.g. managing angry feelings).

An alternative, also suggested by Buchalter (2009), is to *draw your armour*: protection from outside forces. You can then think about how the person has developed or utilised defences (both 'healthy' and 'unhealthy') for particular purposes; for example, to keep others at arm's length or to avoid thinking about painful memories. If you use this technique, you can develop the narrative to increase awareness of these adaptive strategies as well as breaking down barriers to possible change.

STEPPING STONES

✂ Materials

Sheets of A4 paper and cut-out stepping stones. Felt-tip pens.

✎ Process

This is an exercise you can use with young people or adult caregivers, but I will focus in the explanation on working with adolescents. It is an adaptation of an exercise that can be found in Wrench (2016). First, ask the young person to draw himself on a piece of A4 paper – this can be as creative or as simple as time and the young person allow. Put this on the left-hand side. Have the stepping stones in the middle and another blank A4 sheet on the right-hand side.

There are then lots of different possibilities for use in assessment. You could ask the young person to think about how he would like life to be in one, two, five and ten years' time – whatever seems most suitable. For some young people, it might need to be much smaller timescales – tomorrow, next week or in three months. This is called a future vision – prompt discussion by asking questions depending on individual circumstances such as:

Will you be in a relationship? What will your partner be like?

Will you have a job?

Will you be safe?

Will you be in education or training?

How will you be feeling?

He can either draw or write about this future self on the blank sheet of paper on the right-hand side. Explain then that the stepping stones are the steps to achieving these outcomes. What would the young person need to do to get from the present (left-hand box) to the future vision (right-hand box)? There may be different routes across, and it can help to think about a number of alternative pathways to maximise the young person's chances of success. It is about breaking down the steps to make them more achievable and setting the young person up to succeed.

✓ Aims

- To build on self-esteem and self-efficacy.

- To explore future life visioning – where he would like his life to be at some stage in the future and how will he achieve this?

- To problem-solve – to think about the steps to improving a situation, a relationship or simply how to move forward.

- To assess whether the person has a sense of agency or whether he seems reliant on others to meet his needs, solve his problems or identify change mechanisms. Can he take responsibility for making changes in his life or taking action if necessary?

👍 Handy hints

If you are working with a parent or caregiver you can use this technique in diverse ways in assessment. It fits well with restorative approaches, working together: to identify goals and steps to success; to establish whether goals are realistic or achievable; to identify what support or challenge may be needed to achieve positive change.

Examples of scenarios where you might use Stepping Stones effectively could be:

- a parent looking at becoming drug- or alcohol-free

- providing a safe home or safe care for children

- being in a healthy, reciprocal, supportive relationship

- getting into education, training or employment

- building a supportive network.

If you have space to do so, it can be good, especially with young people, to use more active methods. You could make stepping stones out of oil cloth, card or cushions, so the young person can move from stone to stone and from present to future. You can then explore how it feels to 'be' in the future and to be taking steps across the stones.

References

Aber, J., Slade, A. Berger, B., Bresgi, I. *et al.* (1985) *The Parent Development Interview.* Unpublished protocol. City University of New York.

Ainsworth, M. and Wittig, D. (1969) 'Attachment and Exploratory Behavior of One-year-olds in a Strange Situation.' In B. Foss (ed.) *Determinants of Infant Behavior IV.* London: Methuen.

Baynes, P. (2015) 'Changing our ideas about change.' *Seen and Heard 25*, 4, 30–41.

Beck, J. (2015) 'Life's stories: How you arrange the plot points of your life into a narrative can shape who you are – and is a fundamental part of being human'. *The Atlantic.* Accessed on 11/11/2017 at www.theatlantic.com/health/archive/2015/08/life-stories-narrative-psychology-redemption-mental-health-400796

Beebe, B., Jaffe, J., Markese, S., Buck, K., Chen, H. and Cohen, P. (2010) 'The origins of 12-month attachment. A microanalysis of 4-month mother-infant interaction.' *Attachment and Human Development 12*, 1–2, 3–141.

Bellis, M.A., Hughes, K., Leckenby, N. *et al.* (2014a) 'National Household Survey of adverse childhood experiences and their relationship with resilience to health harming behaviours in England.' *BMC Medicine 12*, 72.

Bellis, M.A., Hughes, K., Leckenby, N. *et al.* (2014b) 'Measuring mortality and burden of adult disease associated with adverse childhood experiences in England: A national survey.' *Journal of Public Health.* doi:10.1093/pubmed/fdu065

Binney, V. and Wright, J. (1997) 'The Bag of Feelings: An ideographic technique for the assessment and exploration of feelings of children and adolescents.' *Clinical Child Psychiatry and Psychology 2*, 3, 449–462.

Blaustein, M. and Kinniburgh, K. (2010) *Treating Traumatic Stress in Children and Adolescents. How to Foster Resilience through Attachment, Self-regulation and Competency.* New York, NY: Guilford Press.

Broadhurst, K., White, S., Fish, S., Munro, E., Fletcher, K. and Lincoln, H. (2010) *Ten Pitfalls and How to Avoid Them: What Research Tells Us.* NSPCC. Accessed on 6/10/2017 at www.nspcc.org.uk/globalassets/documents/research-reports/10-pitfalls-initial-assessments-report.pdf

Broughton, C. (2010) 'Measuring Trauma in the Primary Relationship: The Parent–Infant Relational Assessment Tool.' In T. Baradon (ed.) *Relational Trauma in Infancy: Psychoanalytic, Attachment and Neuropsychological Contributions to Parent–Infant Psychotherapy.* London: Routledge.

Brown, L. and Turney, D. (2014) *Analysis and Critical Thinking in Assessment* (2nd edn Handbook) Dartington: Research in Practice.

Brown, R. and Ward, H. (2013) *Decision-making Within a Child's Timeframe. An Overview of Current Research Evidence for Family Justice Professionals Concerning Child Development and the Impact of Maltreatment.* Working Paper 16 (2nd edn). Childhood Wellbeing Research Centre. Accessed on 23/10/2017 at www.gov.uk/government/uploads/system/uploads/attachment_data/file/200471/Decision-making_within_a_child_s_timeframe.pdf

Buchalter, S.I. (2009) *Art Therapy Techniques and Applications.* London: Jessica Kingsley Publishers.

Bunn, A. (2013) *Signs of Safety in England.* An NSPCC commissioned report on the Signs of Safety model in child protection. Available online at www.nspcc.org.uk/services-and-resources/research-and-resources/2013/signs-of-safety-model-england

Cabinet Office, Social Exclusion Task Force (2008) *Families at Risk. Background on Families with Multiple Disadvantages.* Accessed on 26/03/2018 at http://webarchive.nationalarchives.gov.uk/20100407191619/http://www.cabinetoffice.gov.uk/media/cabinetoffice/social_exclusion_task_force/assets/families_at%20_risk/risk_data.pdf

Cafcass and Women's Aid (2017) *Allegations of Domestic Abuse in Child Contact Cases.* Accessed on 26/03/2018 at http://cdn.basw.co.uk/upload/basw_45331-2.pdf

Carey, M. and Russell, S. (2002) 'Externalising – commonly asked questions'. Dulwich Centre. Accessed on 12/8/2017 at http://dulwichcentre.com.au/articles-about-narrative-therapy/externalising

Cavalcante, P. and Mandra, P. (2010) 'Oral narratives of children with typical language development.' *Pró-Fono Revista Atualização Científica 22,* 4, 391–396.

Cavanagh Johnson, T. (1998) *Treatment Exercises for Child Abuse Victims and Children with Sexual Behaviour Problems.* Dover, Kent: Smallwood Publishing.

Dalzell, R. and Sawyer, E. (2016) *Putting Analysis into Child and Family Assessment: Undertaking Assessments of Need.* London: Jessica Kingsley Publishers.

Davies, P. (2000) 'Researching democratic understanding in primary school.' *Research in Education 61,* 39–48.

Davies, W. (2017) *DBT Essentials.* Leicester: The APT Press.

Department for Education and Skills (2005) *Information for Parents: Speech and Language Difficulties.* Nottingham: DfES Publications.

Department of Health (2009) *Improving Safety, Reducing Harm: Children and Young People and Domestic Violence: A Practical Toolkit for Front-line Practitioners.* London: Department of Health.

Department of Health, Department for Education and Employment and the Home Office (2000) *Framework for the Assessment of Children in Need and their Families.* London: The Stationery Office.

Department of Health and Department for Education and Skills (2007) *Good Practice Guidance on Working with Parents with a Learning Disability.* Accessed on 26/03/2018 at http://webarchive.nationalarchives.gov.uk/20080817163624/http://www.dh.gov.uk/en/Publicationsandstatistics/Publications/PublicationsPolicyAndGuidance/DH_075119

De Shazer (2012) *More than Miracles: The State of the Art of Solution-Focused Therapy.* Binghampton, NY: Haworth Press.

Devine, L. (2015) 'Considering social work assessment of families.' *Journal of Social Welfare and Family Law 37,* 1, 70–83.

Dunhill, A. (2009) 'What Is Communication? The Process of Transferring Information.' In A. Dunhill, B. Elliott and A. Shaw (eds) *Effective Communication and Engagement with Children and Young People, their Families and Carers.* Exeter: Learning Matters.

Dunhill, A., Elliott, B. and Shaw, A. (eds) (2009) *Effective Communication and Engagement with Children and Young People, their Families and Carers.* Exeter: Learning Matters.

Dutt, R. and Phillips, M. (2010) 'Assessing the Needs of Black and Minority Ethnic Children and Families.' In J. Horwath (ed.) *The Child's World: The Comprehensive Guide to Assessing Children in Need* (2nd edn). London: Jessica Kingsley Publishers.

Fahlberg, V. (1991) *A Child's Journey Through Placement.* London: BAAF.

Felitti, V.J., Anda, R.F., Nordenberg, D., Williamson, D.F. *et al.* (1998) 'Relationship of childhood abuse and household dysfunction to many of the leading causes of death in adults: The Adverse Childhood Experiences (ACE) Study. *American Journal of Preventative Medicine 14,* 245–258.

Ferguson, H. (2016) 'How children become invisible in child protection work.' *British Journal of Social Work 0,* 1–17.

Ferguson, H. and Norton, J. (2011) *Child Protection Practice.* London: Palgrave.

Fonagy, P., Target, M., Steele, H. and Steele, M. (1998) 'Bridging the transmission gap: An end to an important mystery of attachment research?' *Attachment and Human Development 7,* 3, 333–343.

Forrester, D., Kershaw, S., Moss, H. and Hughes, L. (2008) 'Communication skills in child protection: How do social workers talk to parents?' *Child and Family Social Work 13,* 41–51.

Foundation for People with Learning Disabilities (n.d.) *Communicating with and for People with Learning Disabilities.* Accessed on 5/2/2018 at www.mentalhealth.org.uk/learning-disabilities/a-to-z/c/communicating-people-learning-disabilities

Geldard, K. and Geldard, D. (1997) *Counselling Children. A Practical Introduction.* London: Sage Publications.

Gilligan, R. (1997) 'Beyond permanence? The importance of resilience in child placement practice and planning.' *Adoption and Fostering 21,* 1.

Gilligan, R. (2010) 'Promoting Positive Outcomes for Children in Need.' In J. Horwath (ed.) *The Child's World: The Comprehensive Guide to Assessing Children in Need* (2nd edn). London: Jessica Kingsley Publishers.

Glenn, M., Jaffe, J. and Segal, J. (n.d.) *Trauma, Attachment, and Stress Disorders: Rethinking and Reworking Developmental Issues.* Accessed 16/2/2018 at www.healingresources.info/trauma_attachment_stress_disorders.htm

G-map (2016) *Assessment, Planning and Intervention using the Good Live Model.* Sale: G-map Services.

Grotsky, L., Camerer, C. and Damiano, L. (2000) *Group Work with Sexually Abused Children. A Practitioner's Guide.* California: Sage Publications.

Hamer, M. (2007) *Kids Need…: Parenting Cards for Families and the People Who Work with Them.* London: Jessica Kingsley Publishers.

Harris, P. (2006) *In Search of Belonging: Reflections by Transracially Adopted People.* London: BAAF.

Hasler, J. (2017) 'How Does Trauma Affect the Whole Family?' In A. Hendry and J. Hasler (eds) *Creative Therapies for Complex Trauma.* London: Jessica Kingsley Publishers.

Hendry, A. and Hasler, J. (2017) *Creative Therapies for Complex Trauma: Helping Children and Families in Foster Care, Kinship Care or Adoption.* London: Jessica Kingsley Publishers.

HM Government (2015) *Working Together to Safeguard Children: A Guide to Inter-agency Working to Safeguard and Promote the Welfare of Children.* London: HM Government. Downloadable from www.gov.uk/government/publications

Holland, S. (2004) *Child and Family Assessment in Social Work Practice.* London: Sage.

Holland, S. (2010) 'Engaging Children and Their Parents in the Assessment Process.' In J. Horwath (ed.) *The Child's World: The Comprehensive Guide to Assessing Children in Need* (2nd edn). London: Jessica Kingsley Publishers.

Hopper, J. and Lisak, D. (2014, 9 December) 'Why rape and trauma survivors have fragmented and incomplete memories.' *Time.* Accessed on 11/11/2017 at http://time.com/3625414/rape-trauma-brain-memory

Horwath, J. (2007) *Child Neglect Identification and Assessment.* Basingstoke: Palgrave Macmillan.

Horwath, J. (ed.) (2010) *The Child's World: The Comprehensive Guide to Assessing Children in Need* (2nd edn). London: Jessica Kingsley Publishers.

Horwath, J. and Morrison, T. (2001) 'Assessment of Parental Motivation to Change.' In J. Horwath (ed.) *The Child's World: Assessing Children in Need.* London: Jessica Kingsley Publishers.

Howe, D. (2005) *Child Abuse and Neglect: Attachment, Development and Intervention.* Basingstoke: Palgrave Macmillan.

Howe, D. (2010) 'Attachment: Implications for Assessing Children's Needs and Parenting Capacity.' In J. Horwath (ed.) *The Child's World: The Comprehensive Guide to Assessing Children in Need* (2nd edn). London: Jessica Kingsley Publishers.

Howe, D., Brandon, M., Hinings, D. and Schofield, G. (1999) *Attachment Theory, Child Maltreatment and Family Support: A Practice and Assessment Model.* Basingstoke: Palgrave.

Howes, N. (2010) 'Here to Listen! Communicating with Children and Young People as Part of the Assessment Process.' In J. Horwath (ed.) *The Child's World: The Comprehensive Guide to Assessing Children in Need* (2nd edn). London: Jessica Kingsley Publishers.

Ironside, V. (2004) *The Huge Bag of Worries.* London: Hodder Children's Books.

Jennings, S., Cattanach, A., Mitchell, S., Chesner, A., Meldrum, B. and Mitchell, S. (1994) *The Handbook of Dramatherapy.* Hove: Routledge.

Jones, D. (2003) *Communicating with Vulnerable Children: A Guide for Practitioners.* London: Royal College of Psychiatrists.

Joseph. S., Becker, F. and Becker, S. (2009) *Manual for Measures of Caring Activities and Outcomes for Children and Young People.* London: The Princess Royal Trust for Carers. Accessed on 27/12/2017 at http://static.carers.org/files/2248-yc-outcomes-manual-sb-4047.pdf

Kendall, S., Rodger, J. and Palmer, H. (2010) *The Use of Whole Family Assessment to Identify the Needs of Families with Multiple Problems.* London: Department for Education. Accessed on 11/11/2017 at www.gov.uk/government/uploads/system/uploads/attachment_data/file/181688/DFE-RR045.pdf

Kennedy, J. (2017) *Culturally Competent Practice.* Accessed 15/10/2017 at www.careknowledge.com/resources/special-reports/2017/oct/culturally-competent-practice?utm_source=http://news.pavpub.com/olmgroup

Koprowska, J. (2008) *Communication and Interpersonal Skills in Social Work* (2nd edn). Exeter: Learning Matters.

Leech, J. (2014) *Using Research: Tools to Support Evidence-informed Practice: Practice Tool.* Dartington: Research in Practice.

Leeds City Council (n.d.) *Practitioner Assessment Resource Pack.* Accessed on 30/12/2017 at http://leedschildcare.proceduresonline.com/pdfs/ch_prot_consult.pdf

Lefevre, M. (2008a) 'Communicating and Engaging with Children and Young People in Care Through Play and the Creative Arts.' In Lucock, B. and Lefevre, M. (eds) *Direct Work: Social Work with Children and Young People in Care.* London: BAAF.

Lefevre, M. (2008b) 'Knowing, Being and Doing: Core Qualities and Skills for Working with Children and Young People in Care.' In B. Lucock and M. Lefevre (eds) *Direct Work: Social Work with Children and Young People in Care*. London: BAAF.

Levine, P. (with Frederick, A.) (1997) *Waking the Tiger: Healing Trauma*. Berkeley, CA: North Atlantic Books.

Lippett, I. (1990) *Trust Your Feelings: A Protective Behaviours Resource Manual for Primary School Teachers*. Burnside, South Australia: Essence Publications.

Littlechild, B. (2012) *Values and Cultural Issues in Social Work*. Accessed on 15/10/2017 at https://core.ac.uk/download/pdf/9322950.pdf

Lodrick, Z. (2007) 'Psychological trauma – what every trauma worker should know.' *British Journal of Psychotherapy Integration 4*, 2, 1–19.

Marchant, R. (2008) 'Working with Disabled Children Who Live Away from Home.' In B. Lucock and M. Lefevre (eds) *Direct Work: Social Work with Children and Young People in Care*. London: BAAF.

Marchant, R. (2010) 'Making Assessments Work for Children with Complex Needs.' In J. Horwath (ed.) *The Child's World: The Comprehensive Guide to Assessing Children in Need* (2nd edn). London: Jessica Kingsley Publishers.

Martin, P. (2007) *The Parent's Helping Handbook: A Practical Guide for Teaching Your Child Protective Behaviours*. Armadale, Western Australia: Safe4Kids.

Maslow, A.H. (1943) 'A theory of human motivation.' *Psychological Review 50*, 4, 370–396.

McGaw, S. (2016) *Parent Assessment Manual Software (PAMS 4.0)*. Software with spiral bound Instruction booklet, Parent booklet and Knowledge booklet. Truro: Pill Creek Publishing.

McGaw, S. and Newman, T. (2005) *What works for parents with learning disabilities?* Ilford: Barnardo's.

Melville, L. (2005) *Working with Children and Families, Vol. 2: A Training Manual*. Manchester: The Family Protection Project/The British Council.

Miller, W. and Rollnick, S. (2002) *Motivational Interviewing: Preparing People to Change*. New York, NY: Guilford Press.

Morgan, P. and Goff, A. (2004) *Learning Curves: The Assessment of Parents with a Learning Disability*. Norfolk Area Child Protection Committee.

Morrison, T. (2010) 'Assessing Parental Motivation to Change.' In J. Horwath (ed.) *The Child's World: The Comprehensive Guide to Assessing Children in Need* (2nd edn). London: Jessica Kingsley Publishers.

Munro, E. (2011) *The Munro Review of Child Protection: Final Report – A Child-Centred System*. Norwich: HMSO.

Murray, M. and Osborne, C. (2009) *Safeguarding Disabled Children: Practice Guidance*. London: Crown Copyright.

National Scientific Council on the Developing Child (2015) *Supportive Relationships and Active Skill Building Strengthen the Foundations of Resilience*. Working Paper 13. Cambridge, MA: Center on the Developing Child, Harvard University.

Ncube, N. (2007) *The Tree of Life: An Approach to Working with Vulnerable Children* [DVD]. Adelaide, South Australia: Dulwich Centre Publications.

Nicholls, E. (2005) *The New Life Work Model: Practice Guide*. Lyme Regis: Russell House.

Nicolas, J. (2015) *Identifying and Working with Disguised Compliance in Child Protection*. Practice Guide no. 2. Hove: Pavilion Publishing and Media.

Nicolas, J. (2016) *Home Visiting in Child Protection Cases*. Special Report no. 112. Hove: Pavilion Publishing and Media.

NSPCC (1997) *Turning Points: A Resource Pack for Communicating with Children: Module 5- Practical Approaches*. London: NSPCC.

NSPCC (2014) *Disguised Compliance: Learning from Serious Case Reviews.* Accessed on 19/11/2016 at www.nspcc.org.uk/preventing-abuse/child-protection-system/case-reviews/learning/disguised-compliance

NSPCC (2015) *Assessing Children and Families: An NSPCC Factsheet.* Accessed on 23/10/2017 at www.nspcc.org.uk/globalassets/documents/information-service/factsheet-assessing-children-families.pdf

Oaklander, V. (1988) *Windows to Our Children.* New York, NY: The Gestalt Journal Press.

Ofsted (2015) *The Quality of Assessment for Children in Need of Help.* Accessed on 27/1/2016 at www.gov.uk/government/uploads/system/uploads/attachment_data/file/451036/The-quality-of-assessment-for-children-in-need-of-help.pdf

Ollier, K. and Hobday, A. (1999) *Creative Therapy 2: Working with Parents.* Leicester: British Psychological Society

Omer, H. (2004) *Non-violent Resistance.* Cambridge: Cambridge University Press.

Padesky, C.A. and Mooney, K.A. (1990) 'Presenting the cognitive model to clients.' *International Cognitive Therapy Newsletter 6*, 13–14.

Platt, D. (2012) 'Understanding parental engagement with child welfare services: An integrated model.' *Child and Family Social Work 17*, 2 138–148.

Prochaska, J.O. and DiClemente, C.C. (1982) 'Transtheoretical therapy: Towards a more integrative model of change.' *Psychotherapy: Theory, Research and Practice 19*, 276–287.

Raynes, B. (2003) 'A Stepwise Model of Assessment.' In M.C. Calder and S. Hackett (eds) *Assessment in Child Care: Using and Developing Frameworks for Practice* (2nd edn). Lyme Regis: Russell House.

Reder, P., Duncan, S. and Gray, M. (1988) *Beyond Blame: Child Abuse Tragedies Revisited.* London: Routledge.

Rees, J. (2017) *Life Story Books for Adopted and Fostered Children: A Family Friendly Approach.* London: Jessica Kingsley Publishers.

Rose, R. (2012) *Life Story Therapy with Traumatized Children: A Model for Practice.* London: Jessica Kingsley Publishers.

Ryan, T. and Walker, R. (2007) *Life Story Work: A Practical Guide to Helping Children Understand their Past.* London: BAAF.

Schofield, G. (1998) 'Making sense of the ascertainable wishes and feelings of insecurely attached children.' *Child and Family Law Quarterly 10*, 4, 363–375.

Schonveld, A. and Myko, V. (1999) *Take Care: Safety Awareness and Personal Safety Issues in the Primary Curriculum.* London: NSPCC.

Selfridge, R. and Sokolik, S. (1975) 'A comprehensive view of organisational management.' *MSU Business Topics 23*, 1, 46–61.

Shemmings, D. (2016a) *Frontline Briefing: Attachment in Children and Young People.* Dartington: Research in Practice.

Shemmings, D. (2016b) 'A quick guide to attachment theory: Tips for social workers and practitioners working with children and families.' *The Guardian*, 15 February 2016.

Siegel, D. (1999) *The Developing Mind.* New York, NY: Guilford Press.

Silver, M. (2013) *Attachment in Common Sense and Doodles: A Practical Guide.* London: Jessica Kingsley Publishers.

Squire, L.S. (1987) *Memory and Brain.* New York, NY: Oxford University Press.

Stanley, N., Cleaver, H. and Hart, D. (2010) 'The Impact of Domestic Violence, Parental Mental Health Problems, Substance Misuse and Learning Disability on Parenting Capacity.' In J. Horwath (ed.) *The Child's World: The Comprehensive Guide to Assessing Children in Need* (2nd edn). London: Jessica Kingsley Publishers.

Tait, A. and Wosu. H. (2013) *Direct Work with Vulnerable Children.* London: Jessica Kingsley Publishers.

Tait, A. and Wosu. H. (2016) *Direct Work with Family Groups*. London: Jessica Kingsley Publishers.

Thoburn, J. and Members of the Making Research Count Consortium (2009) *Effective Interventions for Complex Families Where There Are Concerns About or Evidence of a Child Suffering Significant Harm*. Safeguarding: Briefing 1. London: Centre for Excellence and Outcomes in Children and Young People's Services.

Thompson, K. (2016) 'Record of a service using mentalization-based therapy – parenting together to help resolve entrenched conflict between separated parents over their children – with particular emphasis on the impact of the work on the therapist.' *Seen and Heard 26*, 1, 29–41.

Treisman, K. (2017) *A Therapeutic Treasure Box for Working with Children and Adolescents with Developmental Trauma*. London: Jessica Kingsley Publishers.

Turnell, A. and Edwards, S. (1999) *Signs of Safety: A Solution and Safety Orientated Approach to Child Protection*. New York, NY: Norton & Co.

Ullman, M.T. (2004) 'Contributions of memory circuits to language: the declarative/procedural model.' *Cognition 92*, 231–70.

Van der Kolk, B. (2005) 'Developmental trauma disorder: Toward a rational diagnosis for children with complex trauma histories.' *Psychiatric Annals 35*, 5, 401–408.

Van der Kolk, B. (2014) *The Body Keeps the Score*. London: Penguin Books.

Veeken, J. (2012) *The Bear Cards: Feelings*. North Bendigo, Victoria, Australia: Qcards.

Vermeulen, P. (2013) *I am Special*. (2nd edn) London: Jessica Kingsley Publishers.

Wachtel, T. (2005, November) *The next step: Developing restorative communities*. Paper presented at the Seventh International Conference on Conferencing, Circles and Other Restorative Practices, Manchester.

Wachtel, T. (2016) *Defining restorative*. International Institute for Restorative Practices. Accessed on 8/2/2018 at www.iirp.edu/images/pdf/Defining-Restorative_Nov-2016.pdf

Walker (2012) *Systems Theory*. Accessed on 26/03/2017 at https://uk.sagepub.com/sites/default/files/upm-binaries/49393_Walker,_Chapter_One.pdf

Ward, T., Day, A., Howells, K. and Birgden, A. (2004) 'The multifactor offender readiness model.' *Aggression and Violent Behavior 9*, 645–673.

Wilson, J. (1998) *Child-Focused Practice: A Collaborative Systemic Approach*. London: Karnac Books.

Working Together with Parents Network (WTPN) (2016) *Update of the DoH/DfES Good practice guidance on working with parents with a learning disability (2007)*. Accessed on 28/03/2018 at http://cdn.basw.co.uk/upload/basw_102351-10.pdf

Wrench, K. and Naylor, L. (2013) *Life Story Work with Children who are Fostered or Adopted: Creative Ideas and Activities*. London: Jessica Kingsley Publishers.

Wrench, K. (2016) *Helping Vulnerable Children and Adolescents to Stay Safe: Creative Ideas and Activities for Building Protective Behaviours*. London: Jessica Kingsley Publishers.

Subject Index

Author Index